YORKSHIRE'S FORGOTTEN FENLANDS

YORKSHIRE'S FORGOTTEN FENLANDS

by

Ian D Rotherham

Wharncliffe Books

I would like to dedicate this book to Professor Chris Smout and to Professor Melvyn Jones for their support, encouragement and inspiration over many years; also to Joan Butt for her patience and untiring work in drawing maps and helping with the research.

First published in Great Britain in 2010 by
Wharncliffe Books
an imprint of
Pen & Sword Books Ltd
47 Church Street
Barnsley
South Yorkshire
S70 2AS

Copyright © Ian D Rotherham 2010

ISBN 978 1 84563 134

Typeset in Palatino by
Phoenix Typesetting, Auldgirth, Dumfriesshire

Printed and bound in England by
CPI Antony Rowe

Pen & Sword Books Ltd incorporates the Imprints of Pen & Sword Aviation, Pen & Sword Maritime, Pen & Sword Military, Wharncliffe Local History, Pen & Sword Select, Pen & Sword Military Classics and Leo Cooper.

For a complete list of Pen & Sword titles please contact
PEN & SWORD BOOKS LIMITED
47 Church Street, Barnsley, South Yorkshire, S70 2AS, England
E-mail: enquiries@pen-and-sword.co.uk
Website: www.pen-and-sword.co.uk

Contents

Short biography

Professor Ian D. Rotherham, environmental geographer, ecologist and landscape historian, is Reader in Tourism and Environmental Change at Sheffield Hallam University. He is an international authority on cultural and historical aspects of landscapes, especially peat bogs and peatlands, and on fenlands and their history. He has researched and written extensively on both Yorkshire landscapes and their history and ecology, and on those of the fens and other English wetlands. His particular fascination is the transformation, often beyond recognition, of ancient landscapes by human activity. Ian's work on landscapes and flooding has been very widely reported. He also writes and broadcasts on environmental issues, and has regular columns in the *Sheffield Star* and the *Yorkshire Post*, and a phone-in on BBC Radio Sheffield.

Notes about contents and scope:

This book is the account of the unique history and culture of the great fenlands which once typified huge parts of the county of Yorkshire. The great swathes of wetlands ran from the massive upland blanket bogs of the Pennines peat, down through the river valleys to spill out across vast lowland floodplains. It is this latter landscape that the book attempts to re-construct. These were marshes, peat bogs, fens and carrs; huge and fearsome yet productive too, these were contested landscapes. Local people used them and indeed depended upon them. For centuries too, the great landowners and even royalty also valued these expansive areas for their rich hunting grounds. Yet ultimately, as fashions and needs changed, the common people were removed, by force if necessary, and the wetlands were drained. When the political will demanded it, and the technology allowed it, the fens were removed, almost without a trace left. Even the largest sites which remain today, such as Thorne and Hatfield Moors near Doncaster, are but sad remnants of one of England's greatest wild areas. The Holderness Meres and Carrs have utterly disappeared save for Hornsea which was just too great an undertaking to drain. Most of the wet areas of Pickering and of the Vale of York and the Derwent Valley are reduced to a tiny fraction.

Remarkably much of the landscape was still intact only two hundred to three hundred years ago, and a deep cultural memory remained in the late 1800s and early 1900s. But by the end of the twentieth century it was as if the great waters had never been. This book tells the story of this ancient landscape, its people and its wildlife, and ultimately of its demise. We can reconstruct an image of the region centuries ago from the itineraries of visitors and the menus of famously lavish feasts to celebrate great events, and from the household accounts of times past.

This is a story that is rooted in the past but which has a resonance today. Much of this land so hard-won from the great waters is at or below sea level. With global climate change, and the complication of coastal erosion, there is the real possibility that nature will take back what she once gave up. For those who live there or with an interest in this area it will be well worth a read.

Acknowledgments

I wish to acknowledge the guidance and hard work of the editorial and support team at Pen & Sword, the assistance by Joan Butt with the maps, and the use of photographs by Christine Handley. Martin Limbert helped with information sources.

FOREWORD

By Professor Melvyn Jones

It is my great pleasure to write the foreword for this book. Until I read it my knowledge of fenland environments was bitty and incomplete. I had led fieldwork excursions in one Yorkshire former fenland area, carried in my head a vivid description from a seventeenth-century diary and read a short book about a small Cambridgeshire fen from cover to cover. Now, having read Ian Rotherham's *Yorkshire's Forgotten Fens*, I feel that my fenland education is much more complete.

The area where I had led fieldwork excursions was the Vale of Pickering. I remember pointing out to students that the vale was the site of a former proglacial lake, Lake Pickering, emphasizing the location of villages at the junction of the North York Moors and Vale in the north and at the junction of the Wolds and the Vale in the south, and the way the parish shapes all included part of the drained fenland. I also described the Mesolithic site at Star Carr and as the students poured over their OS maps I drew their attention to the almost-ubiquitous place-name 'carr' from the Old Norse *kjarr*, meaning a wooded marsh. I also remember the track that I led students along across the vale as they mapped the agricultural land use; it was known as the 'causey', a raised track above often-flooded land.

The description that I carry around in my head is of the last royal deer hunt that took place in the fens about Hatfield in South Yorkshire in 1609. The description is by the antiquarian and diarist Abraham de la Pryme (1671–1704) and was quoted in the Reverend Joseph Hunter's *South Yorkshire* (Volume 1, 1828: 156). The occasion was a visit to Hatfield Chase of Prince Henry, Prince of Wales. The royal party embarked themselves in almost 100 boats having frightened about 500 deer to take to the water. They pursued them into Thorne Mere, 'and there being up to their very necks in water, their horned heads raised seemed to represent a little wood'. Ian quotes the piece in full in Chapter 2.

The book that I had read from cover to cover is a very short book, just sixty-seven pages. It was Eric Ennion's *Adventurers' Fen*, published by Methuen in 1942. It carries a vivid account of this small fenland remnant over a period of forty years, from 1900 to 1940, during which time it changed from being a working fen (with litter cutting for coarse hay, turf cutting for domestic fuel, reed cutting for thatching and osiers for making wicker baskets and eel traps) to being drained and farmed, then reverting back to nature during the depression years of the 1930s, and then at the outbreak of the Second World War being lost to agriculture forever. As Brian Vesey-Fitzgerald says in his foreword to the book, it is a love story, 'the headstone over the grave of a part of Britain ... where but a short while ago the bittern nested in sugar beet'.

And this quotation says it all. Visitors to former fenland regions today, and the people who live there, see a tamed landscape and are largely unaware of what the fens once looked like, how their resources were exploited for thousands of years, of the rich plant life and animal life that once abounded there, and how they were destroyed. All they see is a rich agricultural landscape. This book tries to set the record straight. It looks at the landscape and wildlife before drainage, the piecemeal and then highly organized drainage of the wetlands and the consequences of the land 'improvement' and then brings the story up to date in the context of twenty-first-century environmental issues.

Ian has been called a 'take-no-prisoners environmentalist'. He has campaigned hard and long for countryside management and environmental responsibility in his native South Yorkshire. Here he takes a wider view and has written a compelling book about a subject that has been very close to his heart for many years. The book has everything. First, it covers all the major former fenland areas in the county: the wetlands of Holderness and the Hull valley, the Vale of York, the Vale of Pickering and – in particular detail – the Humberhead Levels of South Yorkshire. Secondly, it covers a vast sweep of time from the very beginnings of fenland environments, 2,000 years of draining and 'improvement', to their virtual disappearance, and then on to current projects to stabilize remaining fenland remnants. There is also a fascinating chapter on the impact of peat extraction and a powerful last chapter about the future and about environmental sustainability in general. It is a story of great loss, of a great ecological catastrophe, but also a vision for the future, a vision for restoration.

His audience is very wide; it embraces not only the general reader, local historians, amateur naturalists and specialists such as landscape historians and ecologists, but also planners, local politicians and national politicians, indeed anyone who cares or should care about fenland environments and environmental concerns generally.

Melvyn Jones
Kirkstead Abbey Grange, Thorpe Hesley
December 2009

Chapter One

Introducing Yorkshire's Forgotten Fens

Water, Water Everywhere . . .

The Northern Fens of Yorkshire and north Lincolnshire extended across around 3,000 square kilometres or 1,900 square miles (about 400,000 large football pitches) of largely flat lowland landscape. Much of this survived pretty much intact until perhaps 400 years ago and a significant proportion well into the 1800s. So, like in a good detective story, we need to ask both where has it gone and, indeed, 'Whodunnit?'

Cast your eyes over a map of the county of Yorkshire and you will find a great range of wetlands and water-bodies. Many of these are natural, but today most are largely artificial, human creations. From water supply reservoirs to fishponds, from medieval millponds to mineral extraction sites, the region is pockmarked with water features large and small. Yet if you examine closely an old map, even one from, say, the early twentieth century, you find evidence of a former wetter landscape. In the technologically driven and manicured landscape of the twenty-first century much of the water has been inexorably squeezed from the environment. Across the lowlands ponds and meres have been drained, fens and marshes have been 'improved'. In the uplands of the eastern Peak and the flanks of the great Pennine chain the moors and bogs were drained and stripped for medieval peat fuel and then intensively 'gripped' for sheep and grouse farming. The resulting wild uplands are in fact hugely modified from their more natural origins. The evidence of former wetlands can be seen in the

1

landscape through the networks of drains and dykes, through the ranks of rectilinear walls and hedges of the eighteenth- and nineteenth-century improvers, and often through place names associated with the past. Marsh Lane was generally the old road down to the common marsh, Turbary Lane or Peat Pits Lane would have led to the common turbary for peat fuel, Land's End was where land and water met, Willow Garth was the place where willow was grown for basket-making, and there are many others. Lots of areas have names containing Moor and very often this was

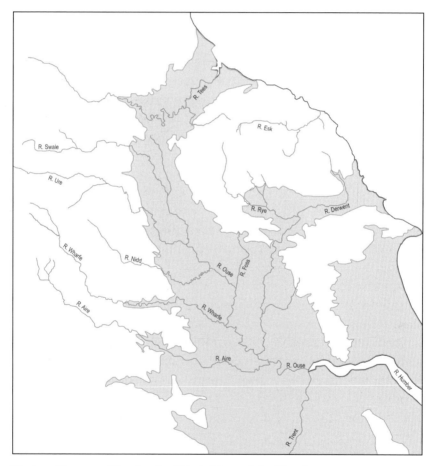

Modern Rivers and Lowlands of Yorkshire and the Humber

the old-fashioned, lowland wet moor such as the Somerset Levels and Moors, not an upland heath.

Stand on relatively high ground looking across a lower-lying valley and you will see the evidence of the former wetlands and also of their progressive loss and ultimate demise. They are all around us, but we have to look in order to see. This book is the story of these lowland wet landscapes and their transformation through the hand of humans, over many centuries. In order to understand the wetlands past, it is necessary to remove yourself from today and the modern living with which you feel comfortable and to immerse yourself in the waters of medieval Yorkshire, be it peat bog, marsh or fen. Only then can you gain some insight into this once vast resource. Even now it is possible to get a glimpse of how this landscape might have looked, perhaps how it functioned, and even of its importance to local communities. Stand in the heart of Thorne Moors, for example, grossly modified though they are by centuries of peat stripping and drainage, and you feel something of the magnificence of a landscape (or waterscape) of unfettered nature. Horizon to horizon, there is no sign of human artefact or construction: today this is an unusual or maybe even unique experience in lowland England. Seek out the great floodlands of Wheldrake Ings near York during a winter flood and you have a tantalizing view of the medieval or even primeval wetlands of ancient Yorkshire. Sadly, though, most have gone and those that remain are tattered remnants of a once vibrant ecology. The greatest challenge today is to restore and repair what is left and even help to reinvent and reconstruct new additions to Yorkshire's fens.

The waters described above did not exist in isolation but were joined by meandering, often sluggish rivers – the living arteries of the vast landscapes of ancient times. These channels gave winter deposits of silts from high grounds to low, providing fertility for summer grazing meadows and for harvests of hay. They provided transportation routes for mobility and trade, they drained the drier lands that surrounded them, and gave back to local people immense supplies of fish, fuel, withies, and much more. Wetlands and rivers also brought fear of flooding and the ever-present spectre of disease, especially of malarial 'ague'. Around the rivers and water-bodies was higher land that was used for farming and for settlement. Even here the landscape past was much wetter than today. Every farming field that you see will have been intensively under-drained for maybe two centuries, the result being a desiccated and increasingly dry landscape and increased flood risk downstream.

The fate of the rivers sits alongside that of the bogs, marshes and fens, as they have been manipulated and constrained and controlled to do humankind's will. Only at times of catastrophic flooding, such as York in 1998 and 2000, do the rivers break out of their artificial channels to once again, albeit temporarily, become the masters of their own horizons. Rivers are straightened and embanked, dredged and drained, culverted, concreted and canalized. Whereas bog, marsh and fen were squeezed dry, the rivers were progressively strangled by generations of engineers charged with bringing order to chaos and productivity and capitalist profit to what was once a common resource. New canals and drains were cut and embanked to take the waters and to provide effective transport throughout the area.

Modern Times

A trip around Yorkshire will reveal a diversity of wet landscapes and wetland features, some natural and many artificial. Natural sites range from the upland Malham Tarn to the great lowland coastal lake Hornsea Mere. The county also boasts many rather distinctive and sometimes downright peculiar sites, such as the lake at Askern near Doncaster. Most obvious to the casual observer are modern wetlands and water-bodies such as Victorian canals and those bringing water supply to industry and drinking water to towns and cities. Alongside these are great wetland sites from mineral working, both naturally and deliberately flooded. Visit Fairburn Ings RSPB Nature Reserve near Ferrybridge, just off the

A1. Here in medieval times there would be vast winter floodlands and extensive summer grazing and meadow. By the nineteenth century came deep-mined mineral coal and the technology of steam power to drain the mine shafts and allow the working of the hidden coal seams. Almost overnight the surface waters would have shrunk as the pumps ushered the groundwater away. First of all the land would have been only seasonally wet, and then quickly all trace of flooding would have disappeared. Yet in some ways this was to be only a short respite. Deep mining of mineral coal includes removal of 'over-burden', or other rock in which the coal is embedded. Brought to the surface, often then with coal fragments and dust too difficult to extract, this material was dumped across the landscape as surface-dominating slag heaps. The result was that even with some back-filling of the cut areas underground, the volume of rock was reduced and the land began the slow process of slumping or subsidence. The result at the surface was the reappearance of so-called subsidence flashes often known as 'ings', or wet fields. By the 1950s these were beginning to appear across the Yorkshire coalfield, usually in places that had formerly been medieval wetlands. Over the next twenty or so years many of these sites were discovered by local birdwatchers to be Meccas for breeding, wintering and migrating birds. It was from these humble origins that some of today's more adventurous and exciting wetland restoration projects began. The Dearne Valley near Barnsley and the Don Valley around Potteric Carr were other locations for such massive fluxes in wetland fortunes.

Other areas such as the lower Swale and Ure Valleys in North Yorkshire were the locations for major winning of aggregates, sand and gravels from ancient glacial deposits. Again, as the sites have run their commercial course they have been flooded, both accidentally and deliberately, to form sites for water-based recreation and for nature conservation. The Swale and Ure Wetlands now form a sort of miniature Norfolk Broads of the north with an award-winning restoration and promotional programme. Some locations such as Killamarsh (in the deep south of the county and once mostly in Derbyshire, and which was the biggest wetland in its area) became largely a derelict and despoiled industrial landscape, to then be aggressively opencast for coal in the 1970s and restored as Rother Valley Country Park. The Upper Dearne Valley north-west of Barnsley came within a whisker of a similar fate but avoided opencast. Wilthorpe Marsh is the final remnant of what must have been a rich and varied valley wetland, but even this was assaulted by the local farmer and his drainage channels in the early 1990s. This is the same story repeated with slight local variants across much of the county over the decades. The Lower Dearne followed the classic cycle of coal mining landscapes as described for Fairburn Ings. Here the once great Ferrymoor, with its low-cost Barnsley 'piggy-back ferry' (where a man carried people across the water), was a source of food and other materials for local people but was drying up due to mine water pumping in the mid-1800s. By the early twenty-first century the process has gone full circle and the RSPB are the now proud managers of a rapidly expanding new wetland landscape. We will re-visit this in due course.

The Former Wetlands and their Fates

So where were the great Yorkshire Fens? Here I need to separate out the uplands from the lowlands because time and space do not permit me to cover both. As hinted already the uplands in the west of Yorkshire and the great expanse of the North Yorkshire Moors were formerly both much more extensive and indeed a whole lot wetter. The changes impacted on the low-lying landscapes in terms of the effects of drainage and desiccation on flooding and on things like habitat continuity and connectivity. However, the story of the uplands is for another time, but whilst we turn to the lowlands and the great and largely forgotten Yorkshire Fens, their intimate relationship to the upper moorland and blanket mires should not be forgotten. Until the 1700s and 1800s the expanse of vast upland moors and bogs stretched often seamlessly down to the valley and floodplains below. It was only with technologically driven agricultural improvement and massive Victorian urban-

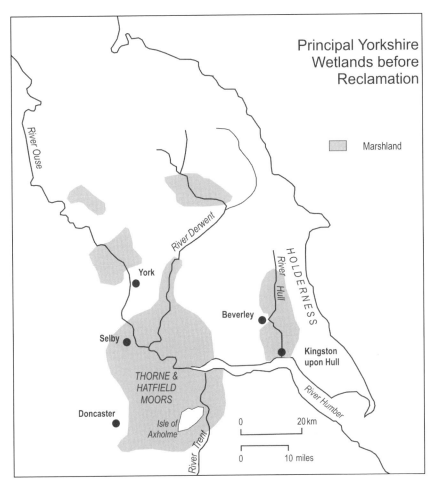

Principal Yorkshire Wetlands Before Reclamation

ization that these areas became totally separated in both fact and in local perceptions.

But this story is about Yorkshire's forgotten fens, and these are mostly in the lower-lying valleys and in the great floodplains beyond. So where were these great wet landscapes, and why did they disappear so dramatically? In terms of location, the medieval fens were dispersed widely across the county. A critical look at landscape and topography can help demonstrate former locations.

After agricultural ploughing, the dark organic or paler silt soils can confirm their once-wet character. The main areas are the vast expanse of the Humberhead Levels in the south and east, the extensive carrs, meres and fens of Holderness, the ancient lake site of the Vale of Pickering, the floodlands of the Vale of York and the Yorkshire Derwent near York, and then the lesser but nevertheless significant marshes, fens and washlands along each of the arterial rivers of the county. Some of the former wetlands and their histories are enigmatic and some are totally lost to us. In particular the Holderness coastline has been rapidly eroding for centuries, at rates of maybe one to three metres per year, much more after catastrophic storms. This, and the varying fortunes of salt marsh and coastal flats around the Humber itself, means that lands have in turn been wetland, reclaimed farmland, and then often ultimately lost back to the seas. How these areas looked and the nature of their undoubtedly extensive wetlands is a matter of conjecture.

Yorkshire's great fens were not alone and isolated. I have already explained the intimate links to the upland wetlands and moors, but the Humberhead Levels in particular were part of a great mass of peat moor, bog, fens, heath and marsh that connected south into Lincolnshire. This area is included within the greater Northern Fen because the boundaries of society and politics have little relevance to the natural landscape.

Unfortunately this is a story very often of destruction and irretrievable loss, of human conflict with nature, and of the long-term consequences of the collective impacts of thousands of individual actions to control and cajole the waters. Much of the loss actually occurred relatively recently, in the last century for example, and most happened over the last 400 years. In telling the story of Yorkshire's forgotten fens I am fortunate to be able to draw on the writings and researches of many workers, academics and amateur enthusiasts over many years, and my then research student Keith Harrison helped in the early stages of mapping and archival work. I will try to acknowledge these as best I can as the story unfolds. Ultimately I am infinitely grateful to all who have gone before and who have each told a part of the overall tale.

A Landscape Transformed

A good starting point is the seminal book by Professor Chris Smout written in 2000, *Nature Contested: Environmental History in Scotland and Northern England since 1660*. This book more than any other helps set the scene on the great Yorkshire fens. It is pointed out that water today behaves in the landscape in ways radically different from how it did in times past. Not only have most of the wetlands gone, but the wider landscape has been drained. So a drop of water falling on a field in, say, Holderness is rapidly shed from the site through an extensive and effective network of field drains. It comes as a surprise to many people that a farmer's field might be little better than an urban concrete surface in terms of absorbing or holding back water in times of flood. Water hardly ever rests on the field surface except in times of severe heavy rain. When the water does stand, then it is generally there only temporarily before it is sucked away into innumerable underground or surface drains. Driven by a demand to 'improve' land for agriculture we have squeezed the living waters away and then progressively developed farmland, roads and homes into the great old fen. Nowadays if major floods re-assert nature's hold, even temporarily, then we have a disaster almost beyond contempla-

Dotterel

tion. But there is a cost associated with this 'progress' and again we will return to this theme later in the book.

It is worthwhile and informative to try and visualize how this wetter landscape might have looked to the medieval peasant or to his or her landlord. Set in an altogether more extensive and expansive lowland landscape would be fens, marshes and seasonal floodlands or washlands. In amongst this, where acid peat accumulated, would be raised peat bogs that might be anything from a few hundred metres to several kilometres across; huge, water-absorbing sponges that shrank and swelled in the landscape with seasonal rains or droughts. On raised acid sands on glacial materials there were extensive heaths and grasslands, and there were widespread wet lowland moors too. Across the whole landscape would be innumerable smaller ponds and pools with associated stands of marsh and fen. Smaller areas of fen and wet woodland called 'carrs' dotted the waterscape with alder (*Alnus glutinosa*) and willow (*Salix* spp.). The arterial rivers that permeated this vast morass of wetland twisted and turned, often back on themselves, creating meanders and cut-off oxbow lakes, again adding to the diversity and wildlife riches of the area. As people encroached upon this largely impenetrable water-world, their early drainage ditches would soon be clogged with rushes and flag and other weedy vegetation. Gradually rivers were straightened, canals and drains were cut and the tide of water-world was inexorably pushed backwards. Drains and embankments, pumps and sluices gradually exerted human technological and political control of the once independent and free waters of nature. By the nineteenth century the engineer and the improver were to hold sway over the waterscape. By the early twenty-first century this change has been wrought so effectively and the transformations etched so deeply into the landscape that there is often little recollection that wetland and fluid nature ever existed. Perhaps the hardest thing is to imagine the wildlife riches of the pristine primeval waterscape or even of the medieval world across the bulk of lowland Yorkshire. There are few records. This is for several reasons and one obvious one is that until a few centuries ago almost nobody could write in order to keep such as record. For such insights as do exist, then, we depend mostly on the itineraries and descriptions of travellers and topographers visiting the areas and viewing it with a foreign eye. We also have diaries and accounts from a handful of educated local residents noted as antiquaries. There is a further problem when we try to imagine the wildlife and vegetation of the region in that until quite late in our story there were no accepted identification or classification systems and few people interested in or able to record and to document the ecology. However, we can get some insight into an amazingly rich natural resource from the account books of houses, halls and great estates and from the records, where they exist, of hunting and of feasting. The results are often almost over-powering. There is a final source of information and this relates too to the unique archival record of the peat bogs that remain. This is through the preserved dead remains of plants and animals embalmed by peat acids and a lack of oxygen, their secrets revealed by teams of palynologists, palaeo-ecologists and palaeo-archaeologists. Professor Paul Buckland, Dr Margaret Atherden, Dr Nicki Whitehouse and Dr Robert Van de Noort have all led teams who have contributed massively to our understanding of the Yorkshire fenland.

A Wetland Lost From Memory

Chris Smout (2000) made the point most eloquently when he stated that:

> It is hard to recall today how much there was once under water. There are many thousands of hectares of what is now prime arable land, especially in northern England, that were in the seventeenth century fen and mire. Considering the fame of the Cambridgeshire, Lincolnshire and Norfolk fenlands, it is surprising how their equivalent in Yorkshire and Lancashire have evaporated from general memory. In

Yorkshire south of the confluence of the Ouse and the Trent, 70,000 acres of Hatfield Chase were 'constantly inundated' before Vermuyden and his fellow Dutch undertakers commenced to drain it in 1626, in an enterprise eclipsed by his achievement at the Bedford Levels in East Anglia.

Smout continues:

At its heart was Thorne Mere 'almost a mile over', the historic bed of which is a modern bone of conservation contention over peat extraction. Potterick Carr, 4,000 acres near Doncaster which fell to Smeaton and his engineers after a private Act of Parliament in 1764, was one of the many outliers generically known as the Yorkshire carrs.

The Holderness valleys were swathed by fens and carrs that opened into salt marsh and flats along the Humber shoreline, with Kingston upon Hull essentially an island surrounded by brackish water and shifting sands. The Julian Dyke and an aqueduct brought supplies of freshwater to the city, but this had collapsed by around 1507 and water had to be brought in by boat. As can be imagined, the excessive cost of this operation for such a basic commodity was a source of much consternation to the inhabitants.

York itself, once the capital of a kingdom, was basically an island between rivers and swamps. The Vale of York with its underlying clays provided excellent summer pasture and meadow but in winter was awash with floodwaters and described by Smout (2000) as 'full of meres and flooded in winter . . . The Derwent in particular was liable to flood at any time of year'. John Leland (Henry VIII's antiquary) in the 1500s described the Derwent as 'this ryver [which] at greate raynes rageth and overflowith', and Daniel Defoe later suggested that it 'overflows its banks and all the neighbouring meadows always after rain'. For modern-day inhabitants of York and the Vale this may sound terribly familiar.

The waterscape was an enigmatic creature which on the one hand provided sustenance, security and even wealth but on the

other hand was potentially fearful, destructive and the harbourer
of disease. Perhaps even more a reason for its ultimate and almost
total destruction was that the Northern Fen was a disputed terri-
tory. It granted a livelihood and potential independence to the
people within it and around it. It did sometimes generate great
wealth for landowners too, and it certainly afforded exotic food for
the feast table as well as sporting opportunities for both aristocrat
and Crown. Yet it was the desire to bring the waterscape into
control, back on to the dry land, and to limit the independence of
local people that was the undoing of the fen. Ultimately their
efforts were harnessed to generate wealth against capital investment for the Church, then the Crown, and eventually for
individual landowners and investors. The final stages during the
nineteenth and twentieth centuries were paid for largely from
the public purse and even by the EU.

But these lands were not unproductive. Smout (2000) notes how
bog hay, a tangle of flowers, sedges, rushes and grasses, could
yield in Scotland somewhere between 12.5 and 19 hundredweights

Wetland Scene

per acre. This provided vital winter fodder for livestock. Wildfowl were abundant, as were fish, and the bogs and fens gave peat fuel, brushwood, flag and sedge, reed for thatching, rushes for candle-making, and on the drier grounds at least, in summer, valuable pasture for livestock. However, this was not enough to save these disputed territories from the hand of the 'improver'. What Smout describes as the 'great reordering of water' was indeed a triumph of the engineer over nature, with spectacular examples being Vermuyden at Hatfield Chase and Smeaton at Potteric Carr. But above all this was a victory at a micro scale for individual farmers and others in a collective and insidious process of field drainage across the land. Strange as it may seem today, this most basic of farming improvements had been problematic for centuries. There had been approaches that had mixed success, with many 'rig and furrow' systems developed to help shed water quickly from the field. Here the water ran off the ridge into the furrow and suppos-edly away along this network of surface drains. The whole process relied on drains joining up and the land having sufficient slope or 'fall' to facilitate the flow. Even without effective run-off the ridges would at least be relatively free draining. Some farmers attempted subterranean drains of loose stones organized into strips or tunnels, and others cut trenches a couple of feet deep, which were then lined with brushwood. However, these systems were gener-ally of only local or temporary success and had a tendency to block and then 'spring' from the ground as a new problematic source of water. The real breakthrough was by the award-winning Joseph Elkington, who pioneered a process of deep trenching at the source of a spring with conduits perhaps six feet deep to take the water away. For total success, though, a further refinement was needed and this was provided by the Scotsman James Smith of Deanston. He addressed the problem of a super-abundance of surface water by laying surface drains in parallel around sixteen to twenty-one feet apart and approximately two-and-a-half feet deep. This was combined with a deep plough capable of breaking the impervious layer or 'pan' that sat underneath many of these wet soils. The final contribution to this revolution in land drainage was by the production and use of cheap and effective earthenware drains. These were first produced in Staffordshire in the Potteries and introduced, for example, into Cumbria some time around 1819. Many landowners subsequently proceeded to produce their own tile drains locally on their estates and the government helped by making loans available at favourable terms to assist the process. An enormous effect of Victorian ingenuity and then sheer hard labour was targeted at this mammoth task of draining the fields and to transform the land. This was probably as significant, if not more, than the highly visible and spectacular efforts of the fen drainers.

The farmers' fields became thoroughly drained, subsoil trenched, and surrounded by networks of ditches, dykes and surface drains to carry superfluous water away. The fields were made uniform, tidied and hedged or walled, and the soils homogenized and manicured. With fertilizers, marl or lime, and – ironically – in many lowland areas irrigation, these former water-scapes became the breadbaskets of the country.

As if buoyed by the efforts of the farmers, the engineers continued their mission of draining marsh, fen and bog. In York-shire Thomas Allen (1828) was lavish with his praise for the Act of Parliament in 1811, which facilitated a further phase of enclosure and improvement around the once intractable Thorne and Hatfield Moors. He noted how 212,000 acres of the 'wide extent of waste' was converted into 'waving fields of corn'. In the East Riding of Yorkshire:

> Within the last half century the vast commons of Wallinfen and Bishopsoil, containing upwards of nine thousand acres, have been enclosed and cultivated, besides several others of inferior extent; and a vast or dreary waste, full of swamps and broken grounds, which in foggy or stormy weather could not be crossed without danger, is now covered with well-built farm houses and intersected in various directions with roads.

Parker and Penning-Rowsell (1980) estimated that there was drainage of about five million hectares of lowland lands in

England during the nineteenth century. It seems that, spurred on by the high prices for corn, the passion for field under-draining peaked about 1840 to 1875. The fall of agricultural prices at this time (1870s) meant that the investment no longer repaid the capital outlay and there was some return to wetter, more waterlogged fields. Across the Yorkshire Fens, the farmland around and in the wider landscape there was perhaps a short-lived breathing space and small-scale local recovery of some wetland habitats. This would be mirrored, as Smout (2000) noted, by increases in birds such as snipe, teal, mallard and redshank, and probably also lapwing and other species of smaller wetlands and boggy fields. No doubt the local populations of frogs, toads and newts would also have thrived. However, this was to be a short-lived reprieve.

The Final Nail in the Coffin

The late Victorian period did little to halt the demise of the greater wetlands but it did slow the impact of farmland drainage and its intensification. The coming of steam power and then other modern energy sources facilitated more effective drainage and water management, and across many areas the Industrial Revolution took its toll. The *Country Gentleman Magazine* noted in 1894 that 'there is not time for the land nearly to repay the outlay before it requires draining again'. This situation continued on and off for the next thirty to forty years, through the Depression years until the outbreak of the Second World War. During and then after the war, all the land abandoned since the Victorian improvers and more besides was reclaimed for agriculture. The efforts went beyond this, and especially utilizing the new technologies of petrol and diesel tractors and tracked vehicles, the farmers and land improvers mopped up the remaining sites left undrained by the Victorians. Innovations in technology allowed landowners to remove marshes, heaths and fens and to drain further and improve both arable and pasture. Simple innovations such as plastic piping made a difference, as did mechanical draglines and the availability of diesel and then electric pumps. There was still an incentive throughout most of this period for farmers to maintain ponds either or both on the farm or in the local village. These were necessary for both watering of livestock and for wetting wooden carts and the like. Since the 1950s there has been a general move towards stock watered by piped water to drinking troughs, with ponds either abandoned or infilled. After the 1980s there has been some limited recovery with the reinstatement of farm conservation ponds.

A result of the process of 'improvement' was the widespread uniformity of the modern lowland farming landscape, at both the wider macro level and within each field too. The pre-improvement landscape was very much a matrix and mosaic of wet and dry, and of differing vegetation or land use at quite intimate levels. By the 1980s this had totally changed to often monotonous improved grassland or intensive arable. There was gradually a slowing of government-funded drainage and improvement schemes, but even up to the 1970s big projects like the reclamation of the Lound and Idle Washlands and Bawtry, in the south of the Humberhead Levels, went ahead. As the remaining sites were recognized as of unique conservation interest, the tide began to turn. Some areas were protected to a limited degree as Sites of Special Scientific Interest (SSSIs) and the legislation eventually tightened its grip on these areas. Other sites, such as Wheldrake Ings, were acquired as protected areas as National Nature Reserves. The Wildlife Trusts and ultimately the RSPB also purchased or were gifted sites. Yet more lands on riverine sites received *de facto* protection as designated floodlands or washlands to hold excess water at times of inundations. These areas were managed by various bodies derived from the old Water Authorities, briefly the National Rivers Authority and now the Environment Agency. Surprisingly it is only relatively recently that many of these areas have moved from management for income generation often by itinerant graziers on short-term leases. Certainly by the 1990s many of the riverside washlands were desperately over-grazed and readily losing biodiversity.

In parallel with the mostly farming improvement described above there were some other distinctive trends in parts of the Yorkshire region. One of the most significant of these, and in the 1980s and 1990s one of the most contentious issues in nature conservation nationally, was the impact of peat cutting.

However, by this time most of the aggressive applications for opencast coal mining had stopped, but a colossal amount of damage had been done. There was also some compensation for the progressive losses with the construction of firstly industrial and other working water-bodies such as reservoirs. Alongside these were ornamental lakes and pools of the great landscaped parks and gardens of rich and powerful landowners, and then of the emerging industrial barons of Yorkshire's towns and cities. Now with a developing network of wetland nature reserves, country parks and created wetlands on former industrial lands, there has been some recovery. However it must be realized that whilst many of these water-bodies are of great value for wildlife and often for water-based recreation, they are different from the areas lost. They are usually less intimately embedded in their landscape, they are mostly deeper and more stable, and often lack the smaller-scale mosaics of habitats and ephemeral waters of the old Yorkshire Fen.

Another major difference between the new and the old is in their relationships with local people. For centuries the Yorkshire Fen was at the heart of its subsistence community and folk made their living and livelihoods in and around the waterscapes. Today where they exist these are mostly leisure landscapes, ornaments to recreation, or they are conservation sites. With this change in ownership, purpose and emphasis there come some long-term problems. All these issues and their histories are reflected in the accounts of the Yorkshire regions and their lost wetlands and fens. Each landscape presents a unique sub-plot but in its way contributes to the totality of the wider story. The Yorkshire agricultural writer and improver William Marshall captured the essence of the issue when describing in the late 1700s how:

In RIVERS, the County under survey is singularly well supplied. The Humber, which might be styled the River of rivers, bonds on the south. The Tees forms its northern confine. The Don, the Air [sic], the Wharf, the Ouse and the Derwent rise in its mountains, and wind through its plains. In commercial light, these rivers are objects of the first magnitude. The tide flows into the centre of the county. Not only Hull, but York, Tadcaster, Ferrybridge and Doncaster, may be called inland ports. The Don is rendered navigable, to Rotherham, Sheffield; the Air, to Leeds, Bradford; the Calder, to Wakefield and up to near Halifax; the Ouse, to Burroughbridge [sic]; the Derwent, to Malton; the Hull, to Driffield, at the foot of the Wolds; and the Tees, to Yarm, on the borders of Cleveland, at the head of the Vale of York.

These great rivers were viewed by Marshall and others as the great conduits of commerce able to link industry and agriculture with their markets. However, they do reflect another characteristic of this vast Yorkshire landscape – for much of its history it was very wet! This very nature of the land was also a great hindrance to early travellers, led to isolation of the wetland communities and caused fear amongst visitors. As Defoe wrote in the early 1700s:

From Rhetford, the country on the right or east lies low and marshy, till, by the confluence of the Rivers Trent, Idle and Don, they are formed into large islands, of which the first is called the Isle of Axholm, where the lands are very rich, and feed great store of cattle: But travelling into those parts being difficult, and sometimes dangerous, especially for strangers, we contented our selves with having the country described to us, as above, and with being assured that there were no towns of note, or any thing to be called curious . . . '

The Northern Fens of Yorkshire and North Lincolnshire

In the early 1960s Alice Garnett, a geographer at Sheffield University, was one of the first authors to write of the 'Humber Fen' and the 'Humber Levels'. She described how the landscape to the east of the exposed coalfield of South Yorkshire changed markedly after the River Don runs through the Don Gorge for around 4 miles, cutting through the dramatic 300–400-foot Magnesian Limestone ridge that runs north–south. At the western end is the great Norman Conisbrough Castle, guarding the strategically important point of the river and of routeways north to south and east to west. This is the land of Sir Walter Scott and of Ivanhoe. Our wetlands lie east of here where the river opens out into a low, broad plain of the Humberhead Levels that remain from the once great proglacial Lake Humber. The land surface is covered by post-glacial deposits of drift or mud (boulder clay) and alluvium from early watercourses that meandered across this vast, featureless plain in prehistory. The consequences for the landscape which evolved over time, until recently, was an expansive, water-logged or wet area with few obvious features to stand out. Most of the land is or was around twenty-five feet or less above sea level, and much is at or around the contemporary modern sea level. Garnett went on to describe the remains of ancient peat bogs, now mostly drained, around Thorne and Hatfield Moors. She notes how over the long period of prehistoric and historic times much of the region was lake or fen, with just a few islands on the Keuper and Bunter sandstones – the hard bedrock – rising above the fenland around Thorne. The only other dry surfaces were on outwash delta deposits of sands and gravels. It was on these rare zones of dry or at least drier land than human settlement was possible. The Roman road north from London diverted to follow these stepping stones across the fen and marsh, resulting in the Roman station at Doncaster being on the lowest solid ground where a crossing of river and wetland could be made. The fenland itself was valued by fishermen and fowlers, and by those seeking respite from persecution and sanctuary from the law. In its later periods, from Saxon times onwards, much of the region was preserved as a hunting chase. This process and the more detailed account of settlement patterns and uses are described later.

The great wetland extended beyond the region called the Humberhead Levels today and beyond that described by Garnett in the 1960s. In the north the fenland extended along the Derwent and Ouse to York, with an outlier beyond in the Vale of Pickering, and up the Hull Valley into Holderness, and in the south it sent fingers of wetland and marsh along the Trent Valley and the Ancholme in north Lincolnshire. Taken together these made up what I describe as the Northern or Yorkshire Fens, and it was really not until the drainage schemes of the early seventeenth century that the region's wetland landscape was significantly changed. The works of Vermuyden and his 'adventurers' (the businessmen and financiers who sponsored his projects), and then of those who followed, changed the landscape from a wetland with the rivers Don, Torne and Idle meandering over a vast flatland between the great rivers Ouse and Trent. The Don was diverted north along the new Dutch River to the Ouse confluence at Goole. The Idle and the Torne were taken into new channels to the Trent north of Axholme. Then with pumping by windmills and the practice of warping, as described later, the land was transformed into one of productive farmland and dispersed settlements and farm-steads. Through the 1800s and 1900s there followed further and more effective drainage of the remaining fens and marshes and the improvement and under-drainage of much of the farmland. This process, as we shall see towards the end of this story, continued pretty much unabated until the 1990s. By the late twentieth century even the memories of this once-great wetland complex had been erased from both corporate and community mental maps of the region. The Yorkshire Fens have been forgotten, but in the light of climate change, flood risk and sea level rise it would be wise to re-kindle our memories of these lost landscapes.

Remembering the Great Inundations

We finish this introduction with a reminder of the risks that affected those who lived in and around the old Yorkshire Fen. The antiquary Abraham de la Pryme described the inundations of the land from the overflowing of the River Don:

> Towards the end of this year [1687] there happened a great inundation on the levels, by means of much rains that fell, and the high tides; which increased the waters so, that they broke the banks and drowned the country for a vast many miles about. My father, and every one in general that dwelt there, lost very considerably in their winter corn, besides the great expense they were put to by boating their cattle to the hills, and firm lands, with the trouble of keeping them there two or three months. I have been several times upon these banks, (which are about three yards in height), when the water has been full to the very tops, and nothing appeared on that side but a terrible tempestuous sea. The water remains about half a week, and sometimes a week, at its full height, whose motions some hundreds of people are watching night and day. But if it chance to be so strong, as to drive away, as it often does, any quantity of any of the banks, then it drowns all before it, and makes a noise by its fall which is heard many miles before they perceive the water; and in places where it precipitates itself down makes a huge pond or pit, sometimes one hundred yards about, and a vast depth, so that in that place, it being impossible for the bank to be built again, they always build it half round, many of which pits and banks may be seen beyond Thorne.

De la Pryme continues with his account of the following decade:

> On the 17th of December 1697, we had a very great snow, which was on the level ground about two foot and a half thick, after a pretty hard frost, which froze over again for several

days. On the 20th it thawed exceedingly fast, upon which there came down a great flood that the like was never known; about forty one years since there was the greatest flood that was then ever remembered, but that was much less that this; for this came roaring all of a sudden, about eleven o'clock at night, on to Bramwith, Fishlake, Thorne, and other towns, upon which the people rung all their bells backwards (as they commonly do in case of a great fire), but though this frightened all to the banks, and bid them all look about them, yet, nevertheless, the loss was very great. The people of Sykehouse and Fishlake, they had banks to save them, yet it overtopt all; drowned the beasts in their folds, and destroyed their sheep; several men lost their lives; the house in Sykehouse and Fishlake being drowned up to the very eaves; so that they reckon no less than £3,000 damage was done by the same in the parish of Fishlake. It came with such force against the banks about Thorne, which kept the waters off the Levels, that every body gave them over, there being no hopes to save them, and ran over them all along, and the ground being so hard they could not strike down stakes upon the tops of their banks, to hinder the water from running over. At last, it being impossible that such vast waters should be contained in such small bounds, it burst a huge gime close by Gore Style, near Thorne, where there had been a vast gime formerly, and so drowned the whole level to an exceeding great depth, so that many people were kept so long in the upper part of their houses that they were almost pined, whilst all their beasts were drowned about them. It was indeed a very sad thing to hear the oxen bellowing and the sheep bleating, and the people crying out for help round about as they did, all over Bramwith, Sykehouse, Stainford and Fishlake, and undoubtedly in other places, yet no one could get to save or help them, it being about midnight; and so many poor people were forced to remain, for several days together, some upon the tops of their houses, others in the highest rooms, without meat or fire, until they were almost starved.

The History and Antiquities of Thorne published in 1829 recounts that since the time of Pryme there had been two or three floods equally as destructive as the one described in 1697. These events each deluged the north side of the River Don and each became a marker of a particular period in the history of the region, and was embedded in the traditions of the local country. Despite the flood banks and the protection schemes this pattern of occasional catastrophic inundation has continued to the present day, and will no doubt do so in the future.

Chapter Two

The Fens of South Yorkshire and North Lincolnshire

A Great Fen

The great expanse of flatland north of the Lincolnshire and Nottinghamshire uplands, east and south of the Magnesian Limestone ridge across South Yorkshire, and south of the higher grounds of the Yorkshire Wolds forms the greatest expanse of wetland in the county of Yorkshire. It was about this area that Chris Smout in 2000 stated how England's third-largest fenland, bordering North Lincolnshire, Nottinghamshire and South Yorkshire, was almost totally destroyed by the early 1900s, the long-term impact of intensive land management and the drainage efforts of Dutch engineers. Potential revenue was the driver for draining much of the lowland fens of England. In 1600 Parliament passed 'An Act for the recovery and inning of drowned and surrounded grounds and the draining of watery marshes, fens, bogs, moors and other grounds of like nature.' The idea developed with James I and was implemented on behalf of Charles I. The build up to and the impact of the drainage of Hatfield Chase have been discussed in detail by Van de Noort (2004). According to De La Pryme in 1699, before drainage of 36,420 hectares of the Humberhead Levels the area was 'A continual lake and a rondezvous of ye waters of ye rivers . . . ' Wilcox in 1933 produced a map that suggested the extent of prehistoric marsh, moss and fen. This was produced nationally but considered only the major lowland floodplains as historically wetland sites. Two maps were produced, one based on geological, topographical and climatic evidence, the other on early literature. The same approach has been adopted for my own studies and for example the maps produced by Darby and Maxwell for their *Domesday Geography* account in 1962 show wetlands and related features (peat and alluvium deposits, fisheries and mills). This helps provide a picture of the once extensive wetland landscape. To understand the nature of these wetlands, it is important to assess and map

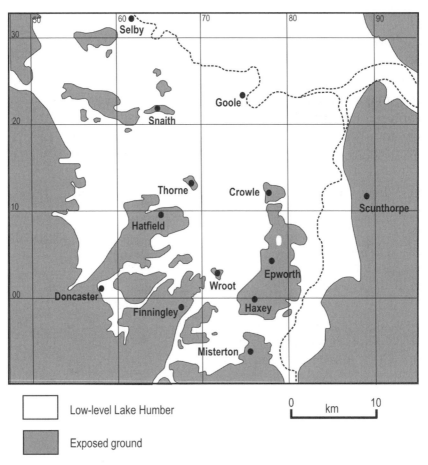

Great Lowlands of the Humber Levels

their extent, and to reconstruct their former ecology. But it is also interesting to try and work out how people utilized them, but this is difficult when so little was written down. So in order to attempt this reconstruction I have accessed early accounts, itineraries and other sources such as feast menus and game books to provide insight into ecology and use.

The now confluent rivers Don and Went, before the Turnbridge Dike, were formerly parts of different river systems. The area was dotted with pools and lakes with the largest being Thorne Mere. Two smaller satellite meres were also present and are seen on Vermuyden's map; though Taylor's study (1987) of the old River Don suggested different locations. The extensive wetlands suggested by alluvial deposits, particularly peat, can be imposed on to maps of the rivers to give an impression of the extensive wet landscape. The Turnbridge Dike is believed to be Roman and the first major change to the region's watercourses by people. This captured the River Went and diverted part of the River Don into the River Aire, perhaps to transport goods and livestock as an extension of routes from the fens to Lincoln. The Dutch drainage obliterated Thorne Mere and the original course of the River Don and diverted several major channels in the area. Agriculture, or generation of capital from sales of land for agriculture, was the driver. The Turnbridge Dike north of the Dutch River disappeared by 1800 and drainage of Potteric Carr, south of Doncaster, took place in the late eighteenth century. Finally, nineteenth-century drainage in the area west of the River Don north of Doncaster almost totally obliterated wetlands, apart from remnants of peat on Thorne and Hatfield Moors. What we see today, though relatively rich and irreplaceable as a conservation resource, is a mere tattered remnant of the once intractable wetland.

The Development of the Humber Wetlands

The evolution of these great wetlands around the River Humber and its estuary has been described in great detail by Robert Van de Noort (2004). This was based on the results of a long-term funded survey of the region's archaeology. The development of the great expanse of fen, bog and carr began around 7,000 years ago with sea level rise and then the effects of climate change. Most significant, however, was the earlier retreat of extensive ice sheets during the warming after the last Ice Age. Furthermore, the underlying geology has a huge bearing on the whole landscape. The bedrock underlying the Humberhead Levels is made up of a series of layers or strata that lie one on another. They dip down under the area and then under the North Sea. The result is a series of higher ridges and scarps such as the Magnesian Limestone immediately to the west and visible in the dramatic gorge where the River Don cuts through the higher rocks. Jurassic marls with sandstones and clays form raised areas east of the sandstones and mudstones of the lower land around Doncaster to Scunthorpe, and the Yorkshire Wolds and Lincolnshire Wolds lie on the higher and more easterly Cretaceous chalk. The latter forms a distinctive west-facing scarp and to the east dips under the glacial deposits of 'till' (mud) covering the lower ground. However, there is a complication that is very important in this wetland landscape. Across all the low-lying areas there is a covering of superficial deposits from post-glacial meltwaters – boulder clay or till, sands and gravels, and then peats from later wetlands. Riverine muds and other deposits also occur in lands prone to flooding or in former river channels. During the last Ice Age the higher Wolds remained ice free, but the lower areas of Holderness, the Hull Valley, the Lincolnshire Marsh, the Humber Gap and the Ancholme Valley to the south were all covered by ice sheets, which left a legacy of boulder clays. The ice extended south to beyond Hatfield Moors, leaving an extensive end-moraine of post-glacial material dumped in the landscape. In the north, just south of York, is evidence of a later phase of deposition as the ice retreated: the Escrick Moraine, with a ridge of till, sand and gravel. The meltwater from the retreating glaciers left lakes in and around the Humberhead Levels and water backed up behind the ice that still blocked the Humber Gap to the east. The result was the extensive Lake Humber, which persisted until perhaps 13,000 to 15,000 years ago, by which time it had mostly silted up. Over the following period the pattern of rivers and streams established in the valleys of the Derwent, Ouse, Aire, Went, Don, Torne, Idle and Trent, ultimately leading to the modern riverine landscape. These rivers flowed eastwards to the Humber Gap to a sea that was around twenty metres below that of today. These rivers meandered to form braided networks of sluggish channels through sands, gravels and muds, the natural banks formed by erosion and movement being reformed by the wind to create extensive sand dunes and areas of coversands. By around 12,000 years ago the climate was warming and sea level rising. In Holderness, of perhaps seventy larger meres that existed at this date in the humps and hollows of the post-glacial landscape, only one, Hornsea Mere, remains today.

Over the period since the landscape structure was laid out, the other key factor that has influenced the wetlands has been the relative levels of the land and sea. The former was influenced by the rising and falling of the earth's surface and especially what is called 'isostatic rebound' following the melting of ice and the loss of the great weight from northern and western parts of Britain. The eastern areas such as the Humberhead Levels and the Cambridgeshire and Lincolnshire Fens have tended to sink over time. Sea level on the other hand varies with climate change and until around 8,000 years ago the whole area was connected by a low-lying land bridge to the low countries of continental Europe. Rising sea level as the waters warmed and expanded submerged the extensive lowlands of the North Sea basin and England was severed from Europe. A consequence of this rapid sea level rise was the development of extensive wetlands across the great expanse the Humber Levels and up the composite river valleys of the region. Robert Van de Noort noted the technical difficulties in producing precise maps of the wetlands of the region because of lack of evidence and the complexities of overlaying of the different periods of incursion and retreat by the sea. However, for the purposes of this account the general story is important rather than the precise technical detail. There were periods of sea level fall for example during the early Roman period and later in the first millennium AD. However, the overall trend has been for sea level to rise and to impede the eastward drainage of the rivers. This has led to flooding outside the main river channel into the floodplains, and also periods of inundation from the sea. The development of the earliest peatlands and also of fens and carrs began around 5,000 years ago. With fluctuating but generally rising sea level the landscape across the Humberhead Levels began to take its modern shape. The zones around the Humber Estuary and the coastal areas developed extensive wetlands of salt marsh and fringing reed-swamp, with alder carrs, sedge fen and on drier ground stands of oak wood and hazel. Along the river valleys the wetlands occupied land between the river and higher areas. The narrowest belt of wetland, about 500 metres wide, was probably along the River Derwent to the north, and the river floodlands along the Ancholme and the Hull were up to 5,000 metres across. However, where the Rivers Torne, Don, Ouse, Aire, Went, Idle and Trent came together in the middle of this vast expansive landscape, they formed a wetland that was perhaps over 200 square kilometres. With further rises in sea level these earlier wetlands were submerged and changed from peat-lands to those dominated by mineral-rich wetlands. These early water-dominated habitats were mostly what are described as eutrophic, meaning that they were rich in nutrients and hence production like reed-beds and carrs. However, over time the deposition of dead organic material from plants built up to raise the land levels above the surrounding water tables. At this point all the nutrients coming into the ecosystem were from rainfall alone and the vegetation developed was what is known as ombrotrophic or 'raised mire'. The two largest areas of this vegetation type were around what are now Thorne Moors and

Hatfield Moors, which evolved over time to become massive raised mires of solid and mostly acidic peat. Underlying the peat on Thorne for example was a forest of large, tall trees that died perhaps as the smaller bogs grew together and made the area too waterlogged for tree growth from around 5,000 years ago. On Hatfield the wooded landscape of alder and birch was overcome by bog development about 4,000 years ago. Over the following millennia the basic landscape evolved from these earlier conditions with periods of growth of peat during wetter conditions and perhaps a slowing or retraction during warmer or drier times. These changes show up in detailed analysis of the peat profiles and in the insect and plant remains preserved in the bogs. Specific markers of climate change occur at 3,260 to 2,820 years ago with a particularly wet period during the late Bronze Age and early Iron Age, then 2,820 to 2,400 years ago with a warmer and drier period in the later Iron Age. This continued through the Roman period but between 640 AD and 980 AD, and similarly from 1250 to 1410 AD, it was wetter. Around 1450 AD, which corresponds to the onset of the so-called Little Ice Age, conditions were very wet indeed. During this period we begin to get historical information too and this suggests a marked period of flooding along the coast and in the valleys of Holderness and the River Hull. Across the region from around the late 1200s to the 1400s there was widespread inundation and increased difficulty in farming lands that had been reclaimed at earlier times.

From the Bronze Age onwards and especially from the Roman period, humans would have increased impacts on this landscape and its ecology. Higher ground would have had woodlands dominated by oak, lime, hazel, elm, pine and ash, with willows and alder. Naturally occurring glades or open areas would have attracted large grazing herbivores and these in turn would maintain and even extend the open habitats. Indeed on areas such as the Holderness Plain the development of early pastoral agriculture resulted in clearance of woodland by around 4,500 years ago. With increasing human population there was pressure on more marginal lands, which included the wetlands. Available skills and technologies limited the impacts that people had in these land-scapes. However, there would have been increasing impacts through the use of fire to burn and clear the forest, to burn grass and heath areas to improve grazing, the selective hunting of herbivores, and probably the indirect effects of hunting top carni-vores and the influences of domesticated animals. There were also impacts from the erosion and downwash of soils and other sediments from above and from limited areas of cultivation. Over the subsequent centuries with periods of social and technical advance, such as during the Roman occupation, and times of retreat and retrenchment, people would gradually make incur-sions into the wetlands through farming improvement and through drainage. At the same time it must be remembered that these expansive wetlands with their arterial rivers and channels would have been hugely important to local people. They provided a rich means to survive in terms of food, fuels and building materials, and they also facilitated quite long-distance travel by boat or canoe.

A Rich Environment for Wildlife and People

Most wetland environments are relatively productive ecosystems, and if they include areas of floodplain and coastal fringe where great rivers spew out their mineral-rich burden of silt and mud they are especially so. This basically means that these can be rich areas for people to live, though the risk of disease and of flooding can make existence hard and precarious. By perhaps 4,000 years ago as settlers moved into this landscape they would have encountered a vast area of mixed wetlands and other habitats with huge but relatively unproductive raised bogs, extensive wet woods of alder and willow, and areas of reed-swamp and sedge fen. The bogs were unproductive and dominated by bog moss or *Sphagnum*, but the other areas were rich in fish and in wildfowl. The regular inundation from rivers and from the sea in coastal zones would have created high fertility and so encouraged even greater biomass and productivity. The people in and around these wetlands would have hunted a diversity of mammals and birds, they would have gathered plants, herbs, fruits and nuts, and they would have caught fish. To the east around the Humber Estuary and along the Holderness and Lincolnshire coasts were mudflats, tidal creeks, salt marshes and extensive sand dunes. In the coastal and estuarine areas they would have fished and caught or gathered shellfish and crustaceans such as crabs and shrimps. It is also likely that the early hunter-gatherers migrated perhaps seasonally and as conditions allowed or necessitated between the different zones. Movement between the lower wetter grounds and the drier uplands would have been necessary, as the floodwaters covered the landscape and people also followed herds of wild mammals that they hunted – both classic strategies of semi-settled hunter-gatherers. Evidence from more northerly sites such as Star Carr in the Vale of Pickering suggests that these people hunted and ate red deer, roe deer, elk, aurochs, pigs and many smaller mammals too. It is likely that they also took beaver and wild boar for food, and mammals such as otter,

Pike

marten, polecat and wild cat for fur. The early settlers also burnt areas of reed-bed probably to increase productivity and perhaps to open up areas of vegetation in the landscape. Though not certain, it is likely that these peoples began to domesticate animals perhaps 6,000 years ago, and were carrying out some limited agriculture by about 4,000 years ago. So during the Neolithic and the Bronze Age the area probably had stock-breeders with cattle or sheep and these would have been in part pastured on extensive salt marshes around the estuary and on the more extensive salt marsh areas across the floodland at that time. By the later Bronze Age and early Iron Age there was more exten-sive arable cultivation across the region around the wetland fringe, and the evidence of pollen analysis suggests large-scale woodland clearance at this time. It is from the late Iron Age and into the Roman period that more intensive and socially organized settlements and associated field systems appear in the higher grounds of, for example, the Lincolnshire Wolds or on the Sherwood sandstones to the south-east. Settlements also appear on the valley floodplains marked out with double ditches and rectilinear enclosures, and with associated drove-ways appar-ently for moving stock from summer grazing on the marshes to overwinter on higher and drier ground.

During this period it was one thing to live around the fringes of a great wetland, but another to live within the wetland itself. However, as already noted these landscapes are productive and also facilitate relatively easy travel over distance along river channels. Wetlands also provide a degree of security through their inaccessibility, particularly for outsiders, and also in that they may have been marginal zones beyond local social and polit-ical controls. They therefore provided opportunities perhaps not available on the wider areas of drier ground. However, even those living in the heart of the wetlands actually settled on the limited islands of higher land or on areas of deposition of more solid substrate, and not in any form of lake settlement as found elsewhere in Britain. The major archaeological site at Sutton Common, once thought to be a prehistoric lake settlement, was most likely a Romano-British grain store. The communities that settled here were also skilled in metal smelting and working with iron from bog ore. This was probably smelted from locally made charcoal from coppiced woodlands of hazel. There is extensive evidence from slag heaps and other features found in the region of Holme-on-Spalding-Moor and in the Vale of York. Log boats loaded with iron presumably for trading have been found preserved in the sediments. Another skill used by some of the local people along the coastal and estuarine zones, certainly by the late Bronze Age and particularly from the Iron Age into the Romano-British period, was salt making. Sea water was evaporated by the heat of the sun and then brine was heated or boiled to produce salt crystals. The salt obtained could be used for preserving food such as fish, meat or dairy produce. It was also used in medicines and in dyes, and consumed as a food additive.

With such activities it has already been noted that from an early time the wetlands were traversed by boat. Prehistoric log boats and sewn plank boats have been found at sites across the region. Some of these were quite sophisticated in construction and imply that the people of the wetlands travelled across the levels and both up and down stream along the rivers, as well as perhaps further afield. Van de Noort notes that these craft may have represented quite significant innovation and design around the Humber Estuary, and it has been estimated that some of them might have carried up to twenty-two cattle or over a hundred sheep. The most commonly used boats, though, were dugout canoes hollowed from a single oak trunk between eight and sixteen metres in length. Such boats have been found in wetlands across the region from the Vale of York to the lower wetlands. One was even found in the sediments of 'Lake Meadowhall', close to where the M1 motorway now runs just east of Sheffield, and is now in Weston Park Museum. By late Neolithic or early Bronze Age the people of the Humber region were trading across the North Sea and into Europe, as well as across the great estuary of the Humber and inland too.

When the Romans arrived in Britain they brought skills,

cultures, technologies and the social and political systems to change approaches to land management, including drainage and reclamation. Around the Humberhead Levels they imposed new roads, bridges, farms and an expansion of settlements into the wetlands. At the same time the sea level was dropping and extensive areas of coastal marsh, for example, were open to colonization and use. The situation was reversed by the later times of the Roman occupation, with the sea once more moving inland. Buckland (1979) has suggested that Romano-British farming on the higher grounds around the Levels led to downwash of soil into the wetland areas. Van de Noort on the other hand attributes this and the subsequent decline in farming through environmental degradation to be in the more immediate vicinity of the lowland wetland zones. Ermine Street was one of the most important Roman roads and led from London to Lincoln and on to Winteringham on the Humber, and Roman forts were built and subsidiary Roman roads crossed the region by around 50 AD. Just as earlier cultures had constructed floating wooden causeways across the marshland so the Romans built 'floating roads' on cut timbers and covered with turves.

There were Roman villas around the region and the wetland fringes were probably exploited as a part of the Roman estate system. Along with Roman forts there were many non-military settlements across the Humberhead Levels, often on the riverbanks of the main arterial rivers. It is likely that the region was exploited for salt making and for pottery, and there was extensive rearing of sheep and cattle. The rich pastures of the riverine floodlands would be used to fatten stock, and the rivers themselves could be used to transport animals and meat. It has been suggested that Brough on the Humber Estuary was a major Roman port, and the towns of Doncaster, Lincoln and York were all important. By the medieval period it was from these larger settlements on the drier ground and a network of smaller villages and hamlets on the islands and other areas of drier ground that much of the exploitation of these wetlands was undertaken. To some extent during this time there was a withdrawal of settlements immediately within the wetlands probably due to social and economic changes in the post-Roman period. The other factor was probably the re-wetting of areas as sea level rose once more. Nature played a leading role in the extent to which people could cultivate and exploit these lands. It seems that the human population in the region decreased and its impact on the wetlands was also reduced. In particular there was a re-establishment of woodland in many areas, probably with oak re-colonizing abandoned farmland. The farms that remained were probably rather self-sufficient in contrast to those of the Romano-British period, and would have been based on the higher and drier land with seasonal use of the wetland fringe for pasture and for hunting and fishing. Then, as new cultures settled, a process of gradual re-colonization began during the Middle Ages. It seems that in the East Anglian Fens and other areas this happened from around 600 to 700 AD, but later in the Humber due to local conditions. Some marginal settlements have been found from this period and give some clue as to the nature of the land use, with arable cultivation but also evidence of geese, chickens, cattle, sheep, goats and pigs. These all suggest the wetland margin was very productive. The communities were fishing and hunting, including wildfowling, and there were signs of shellfish such as oysters being taken, and even dolphin or porpoise, and whales were consumed, though obviously from further afield. Having been colonized by the Anglo-Saxons in the post-Roman period, from the late 800s the whole region was part of the area controlled under the Danelaw with widespread settlement from Scandinavia. One of the main consequences in the modern-day landscape is the large number of settlements with Viking names, although many settlements retained strong Saxon influences.

Settlement in the Yorkshire Fens

Across the fenland the Middle Ages settlements were mostly on higher or at least drier ground. These included areas of drier glacial deposits or the raised banks or levees along rivers. Essentially these were small islands of settlements in a wider sea of wetland. It is suggested by Van de Noort the reclamation of the marsh may have begun before Domesday in areas such as around the Trent and the Ouse with the protection of key settlements from extreme high tides by defensive banks. Colonization followed and land was drained by long dykes to facilitate cultivation and/or building. A sea-bank was built along the tidal Ouse by the late 1000s and in its lee sheltered a series of settlements. By the time of Domesday there were parishes often with multiple settlements recorded as communities edged their way into the fens. Along the coastal zones was an eastward movement of satellite townships linked to the need to be close to the sea for the important local industry of salt manufacture. After the Norman Conquest there were a number of motte and bailey castles built across the region, controlling access to, across, or along major waterways. Large areas of the Humber wetlands and associated areas were taken from Saxon nobles and given to Norman overlords, and it was from these castles that they controlled their new acquisitions. Owston Castle for example was built to control the strategically important cross-Trent ferry and therefore access to the productive Isle of Axholme.

An important consequence of the Norman Conquest for the region was the imposition of Forest Law across much of the area and the establishment of hunting chases. In 1311 the Lord of Axholme, John de Mowbray, established a free chase in his manor and soke of Crowle and retained this in a grant to Selby Abbey. Across the chase at Hatfield hunting, farming and woodland use were all carefully controlled. Around thirty-four parks and hunting forests have been recorded across the region and it is very likely that there were more. The area was indeed a landscape famous for its deer and its hunting. Furthermore, these lands were rich hunting grounds and this often gave them a degree of protection from agricultural improvement. Conisbrough Castle Park in South Yorkshire may have early origins as an Anglo-Saxon hunting area. Then from shortly after the Norman

Conquest to 1347, 70,000 low-lying, often inundated acres of Hatfield Chase were the private forest of the de Warennes of Conisbrough. According to *The History of Thorne* the Earls of Warenne had a house close to Hatfield in the centre of the chase where they could stop and rest when away from their seat of Conisbrough Castle. The house also had a park of 500 acres, which was well stocked with deer, though they were also 'to be seen roaming at large through the whole limits of the chase'.

The chase then reverted to the Crown in 1347 and Forest Law was applied to Hatfield Chase. This meant the royal forest law, with the threat of punitive treatment of offenders who transgressed the strict protection for game. In practice this was more often a means of raising royal revenue than of punishing people. Vernon Cory, writing in 1985, described the great chase of Hatfield as the largest deer park in England, covering 72,850 hectares or 180,000 acres. Technically it wasn't a park as such, but a hunting chase. The central hunting area was termed 'soft land' with 'hard land' beyond the chase, which keepers could enter in order to retrieve game. There was also hunting outside the chase itself in districts called 'purlieus' and within which Forest Law did not apply. Apparently Selby Abbey kept a keen interest in these areas, the clergy of the time being notable for their sporting interests. Cory estimates the deer population to have been around one deer per twenty-five hectares or sixty-two acres, which is not particularly dense. There were both red and fallow deer, though it is suggested that the fallow were restricted to Conisbrough Park.

When in 1356 Edward Balliol, the ex-king of Scotland, resided at Wheatley near Doncaster he received a pardon for the slaughter of deer he had committed. This is documented as sixteen hinds, six does, eight stags, three calves and six kids, all in the chase. In the park the slaughter continued further, with eight damas (fallow deer), one souram, one sourellum (a kind of fallow deer), and in the ponds two pikes of three-and-a-half feet in length, twenty of two-and-a-half feet, twenty of two feet, fifty pickerels of one-and-a-half feet, six of one foot, one hundred and nine perch, roach, tench and skelys, and six breams and bremettes. The bailiff of Hatfield was Robert de Mauley and his lieutenant was John de Aldwick. The harvest reaped bears testimony to the rich wildlife of this landscape and well as to the hunting prowess or at least perseverance of the former Scottish king.

There was a regular and ongoing use of the area for fish and game, but it seems that great hunts were relatively infrequent. One was noted by Vernon Cory as recorded in 1541, during the reign of Henry VIII, when 200 stags and does were killed in a single day. In 1607 it held red and fallow deer, once as common 'as sheep upon the hills', and 'so unruly that they almost ruined the country'. The inquisitions of 1607 stated that 'the number of red deer amounts to about a thousand, and that the herd is much impaired by the depredations of the borderers'. Poaching was common and offenders might be gaoled in Thorne Castle and/or fined, the latter being a useful way of raising revenue. The management of the chase was overseen by the king's Bow Bearer, a title that later became the rather less extravagant Surveyor General. Beneath him were the Master or Chief Forester, five Keepers (for the wards of Wroot, Hatfield, Broadholme, Clownes and Wrangles), and twenty-five Regarders (to control the bounds of the forest and who attended the forest court). The last documented major hunt occurred in 1609, the royal party in 100 boats pursuing 500 deer across Thorne Mere. This tale was described by Abraham de la Pryme:

> When Henry Prince of Wales visited Yorkshire in 1609 he was entertained at Streethorpe on the side of the Chace towards Doncaster, the residence of Sir Robert Swift. After one day spent in plain stag hunt the chief regarder of Thorne and R. Portington esquire having promised to let the prince see such sport as he never saw in his life the prince and his retinue went with them; and being come to Tudworth, where Mr. Portington lived, they all embarked themselves in almost 100 boats that were provided there ready, and having

frightened some 500 deer out of the woods grounds and closes adjoining (which had been driven there the night before) they all as they were commonly wont took to the water and this royal navy pursuing them into that lower part of the levels called Thorne Mere and there up to their necks in water their horned heads raised seem to present a little wood, and there being compassed about with the little fleet, some ventured among them, and feeling such and such as were fattest, they immediately cut their throats and threw them up into the boats or else tying a strong rope to their heads drew them to land and killed them. Having thus taken several they returned in triumph with their boats to land and the prince dined with R. Portington esquire and was very merry and well pleased at his day's work.

In 1609 Prince Henry the Prince of Wales was only fifteen years old. However, to put this in perspective, at that time he could well

Prince Henry Slaying
Red Deer

have been considered as a young adult. His story is very pertinent to the rest of the account and indeed to the future of the Yorkshire Fens at that time. He was the elder son of James I and was being groomed to succeed him, even when James was only James VI of Scotland and not yet king of England. Yet as Martin Taylor notes, Henry was not a traditional name for a Scottish king, and it may be that he believed he was naming the future English monarch. So when James succeeded to the English throne on the death of Elizabeth I, Henry was next in line. However, in 1612, Henry died. His is perhaps one of the most significant deaths in English history. If he had not died so prematurely then it is considered by many historians that the collapse into civil war would never have happened. It is likely that at least the relationship of tolerance with the House of Commons that was developed by his father, James I of England, would have continued, and maybe a more fruitful partnership would have evolved. Roy Strong describes Henry as 'a young man of exceptional promise with a passionate interest in the arts and a commitment to revive the vanished glories of the previous reign'. This was not to be. He died of typhoid fever at the age of nineteen. Then on the death of James I, on 27 March, Henry's younger brother Charles succeeded to the throne and the relationship deteriorated to civil war, the trial and beheading of the king, and the short establishment of the Commonwealth with Oliver Cromwell as the Lord Protector. One can only wonder what the fate of our Yorkshire fenlands might have been if Henry had survived. The country and the Crown in particular would probably not have descended into near anarchy and financial chaos, and as a lover of the hunt it is likely that he would have preserved at least Hatfield if not other wetland areas. As it was, Hatfield Chase, famous for its fisheries and swans, was disforested in 1629 and drained in the early 1630s. When the chase was disforested the deer were mostly captured and transported to other parks. However, they were not all removed immediately, as on 30 December 1634 John Scandaren was paid £100 for bringing forty red deer alive from Hatfield Chase to stock Burley Park, Oakham.

Peat spade

The other major and important consequence of the Norman takeover of this landscape was the establishment or sometimes re-establishment of a monastic system. This had huge implications for land reclamation and exploitation, and therefore for re-colonization. Selby Abbey was established by William the Conqueror, also known as William the Bastard. The abbey had large land-holdings across the region and it was in these that the first large-scale co-ordinated reclamation took place. Their works included the digging of drains such as the aptly named Bishop's drain in Selby during the late 1000s and early 1100s. This is shown as encircling the great Thorne Moors on the Inclesmoor Map from circa 1405 AD. Reclamation included the building of roads, drains and bridges, with the founding of villages and the erecting of crosses. Peat fuel was dug on a large scale, by working into the peat bog from the edges, resulting in long linear strips with a drain down each side and known as 'moorland allotments'. These features, highlighted by Keith Miller of English Heritage, actually survive in the landscape today as a major and distinctive feature and the process of peat bog reclamation exactly mirrors that undertaken in the flatlands of Holland and Germany. Linked to Selby Abbey were a number of monasteries and priories established across the area during the 1100s and 1200s, and it was through these that much of the work was undertaken. At least forty ecclesiastical centres are known within the Humberhead Levels and others outside the immediate area held lands here too. This network was the foundation for the process of land reclamation and improvement here as it was in the East Anglian Fens. Van de Noort also raises the interesting concept that this was seen as the 'conversion' of waste as a parallel to the spiritual conversion of pagans to Christianity. Land improvement increased tax revenues and the value and wealth of the Church and the region. Indeed the great wealth of the ecclesiastical centres was based largely on wetland exploitation delivered and managed through a dispersed estate of monasteries. These centres would not only have farmed the land but also managed fishponds and small industries.

In the post-Domesday period a network of towns and villages began to re-emerge, though many Roman settlements had been largely abandoned after the collapse of the Roman Empire. The new towns were sometimes on these earlier sites and centres such as Doncaster began to grow alongside newly established towns such as Beverley. With increasing populations and a number of urban centres there were further demands on the landscape of the Levels, and many areas had extensive 'commons' across the region. Those at Beverley are notable survivors to this day. Further hunting forests (such as at Selby) and parks were also established. This process helped speed the work of reclamation and agricultural improvement with extensive drainage schemes across the wetlands. The farmers of the Yorkshire Fens were once again connected to the economy and society of the wider area. In some parts of this fenland the work was encouraged by the establishment of new moated settlements in lands not yet exploited by nearby villages. Some of these moated properties were farms or monastic estate buildings, and others were the houses of nobles, suggesting that both Church and nobility were involved in this process. In this wet landscape the moats probably helped lower the water-table immediately around the site and thus helped maintain the land inside the moat higher and drier. By this time the arable land on slightly higher and drier ground was worked as townfield with open strip fields aggregated around a nucleated settlement. These areas included the small islands such as Holme-on-Spalding-Moor, Axholme and Wroot, on adjacent hillsides and along raised levees by the main rivers. In the lower wetter areas were common meadows on the mineral-rich floodplains; important and productive resources and often called 'ings'. These lands provided summer grazing and also the important stock of hay for the winter months, both important for livestock and oxen for ploughing. Remaining beyond these areas were the true wetlands of the Yorkshire Fen. These included wet woodlands or carrs, moors and 'wastes' with high water-tables and peat for-mation. When water levels allowed, these areas could be exploited as grazing pasture and as part of a complex system for managing this vast landscape. The wetland grazing enabled the higher ings to be set aside for a few months to produce hay. The hay was cut and the stock could then go back on the ings, and winter floods then brought fresh deposition of mineral-rich sedi-ments to these riverside fields; the whole system maintained and sustainable. On some of the common wastes the local villagers were recorded as keeping cattle, draught oxen, horses, sheep, pigs and geese.

Turbaries and Turves

Some of the wetlands such as Askham Bog, Tillmire and Skipworth Common close to York were known to be turbaries in Roman times, supplying peat fuel to the city of York and perhaps to other Roman garrisons. However, by the medieval period the use of the Yorkshire Fens for the supply of peat fuel was well established as a major operation. Not only was peat turf used for fuel but also for building. The best known example is at Thorne Moor or Thorne Waste, where by the 1200s and 1300s a major industry was established. The famous Inclesmoor Map shows clear evidence by the 1400s of arterial drainage, roads, bridges and peat cutting turbaries. The ecclesiastical centres probably led this process of exploitation as they did in Norfolk to supply the cathedral at Norwich. The fuel was used for domestic heating and for cooking at the great institutions and in smaller farms and cottages. However, it was also used to power industries such as potteries, brick and tile making, even salt manufacture. Along with the peat there was also a harvest of 'bog oak' with prehistoric timbers preserved in the peat. Heavy and durable, these black timbers impregnated with tannins could either be a premium fuel or used in building as documented for the bogs of Ireland. Some from Hatfield Moor were even sold as ships' masts. As the turbaries were exploited the water-table was lowered and the land remaining became available for cultivation. If the water-table rose then locally turbaries would be flooded and abandoned. Exploitation for peat continued throughout the centuries up to the present day.

A Land of Lakes, Pools and Meres

In the most low-lying areas there was open water. This might be along the major rivers or around the estuary in smaller pools, meres and lakes (although some really quite large). Again, within the overall management of this landscape complex, the water-bodies were important. Along their fringes could be harvested reeds and sedges for thatching and sometimes for fuel, and for basket-making. Small willows or withies would be harvested in osier holts or willow garths, again for construction or for basketry. These pools also supplied fish and the rights were held by local towns or by the monasteries. The tidal rivers had fish weirs to catch eels and other migratory fish. The Domesday Book in 1086 notes that at Tudworth in the Humberhead Levels there

Marsh Marigold

CALTHA PALUSTRIS.   MARSH-MARIGOLD. *Y.*

were 20 fisheries producing around 20,000 eels each year. There is documentation of payments to monasteries being in fish from the fishponds and especially in eels. Across the Yorkshire Fen, wild-fowling was hugely important, with birds trapped in nets and driven when flightless across the ponds and meres. The duck decoy, a purpose-built pool with traps to catch wildfowl, was to follow as a later invention, but at Leconfield Castle in the Hull Valley, mallards, snipes, curlews, redshanks, plover and swans were all caught and eaten.

Productive Landscapes

The wetlands provided fish, reed and rushes (for thatching, flooring and candles), peat fuel, brushwood from the carrs for fuel and light constructional work, and pasture for cattle. As Smout notes, it was not only the marshes and meres of Yorkshire and Lancashire that had economic value for people, but the same was true of wetlands across northern Britain. In the accounts of John Leland there is a description of the feast for the enthronement of George Neville as the Archbishop of York in 1466. This may have a degree of exaggeration, and much of the food would have been supplied from the Derwent Washlands, south of York. Nevertheless, it does give insight into the likely wildlife at the time in the South Yorkshire and Humber marshes and fens:

> Oxen 104; Wild Bull 6; Muttons 1,000; Veales 304; Porkes 304; Piggs 3,000; Kidds 204; Conyes 4,000; Staggs, Bucks and Roes 504; Pasties of venison cold 103; Pasties of venison hot 1,500; Swans 400; Geese 5,000; Capons 7,000; Mallard and Teal 4,000; Plovers 400; Quails 100 dozen; Fowles called Rayes 200 dozen; Peacocks 400; Cranes 204; Bytternes 200; Chickens 3,000; Pigeons 4,000; Hernshawes [young herons] 400; Ruff 200; Woodcock 400; Curlews 100; Pheasants 200; Partridges 500; and Egritts 1,000.

Other regional household accounts confirm cranes, herons, snipe, bittern, quail, larks, dotterel and bustards for the table (1526), peacocks, cranes and bitterns (1530) and twelve spoonbills at 1s each, and ten Bitterns at 13s and 4d (1528). Many are wetland birds and mammals from forest or chase; these were extensive, productive landscapes. Little bittern, night heron and purple heron probably survived in English wetlands until the 1600s. Cranes and spoonbills were extinct as breeding birds in England for around 300 years, but ruff bred at Hatfield Chase until the 1820s. Thomas Pennant in 1766 described taking ruff in nets, fattening in captivity and selling them for the table at 2s each.

New techniques in wildfowling were important, before modern guns. The Dutch duck decoy came in the 1600s, with Dutch drainage engineers. Thousands of wildfowl were captured every year from South Yorkshire's fens. Even Doncaster Corporation had a duck decoy, paid for as an investment or from money for

Bittern

the upkeep of the poor. Making the decoy and a special embankment, the 'Decoy Bank' (over three-quarters of a mile long), to
reach it cost £160. The decoy pond was circular, with six-and-a-
half acres of water and six 'pipes' (to collect ducks!). In 1662 it was
let for twenty-one years at an annual rent of £15, which fell in 1707
to only £3 per year, perhaps reflecting the impact of drainage. The
lessee of 1707 specialized in pochards, one of the best ducks for
the table, by nets raised by pulleys on poles after the birds settled
on the water. All the duck pipes were still there in 1778. The last
decoy man died in 1794, and by the late 1800s the Great Northern
Railway ran straight through what had been the decoy.

For over 200 years the pressure has been to tame this wilder-
ness and to 'improve' the land and its productivity. Cobbett in
1830 described the lands reclaimed from the Humber area as
(with the exception of the Cambridgeshire fenland) the richest
and most fertile he had seen in the whole of England. The value

Shooting wild duck

of land at Hatfield Chase was raised from 6d per acre to 10s by the Dutch improvers. This was the value to the farmer and landowner and does not reflect that to the community living and working in and around the wetlands. But from this time on the areas around Potteric Carr were turned increasingly to agriculture, to industry with coal mining and railways, and to a suburb of the emerging urban areas of Doncaster. Thorne and Hatfield Moors, at the core of the great Northern Fen, were increasingly surrounding by intensive agriculture and again affected by industry, both coal and peat extraction. By the late twentieth century barely any recollection remained of the once great wetland that dominated the entire landscape: truly a forgotten fenland.

Chapter Three

The Wetlands of Holderness
and the Hull Valley

the most that I find remarkable here is that there is nothing
remarkable . . . for above thirty miles together; not a port, not a
gentleman's seat, not a town of note.

Daniel Defoe on the Holderness coast in the 1720s

A Vanished Waterscape

Interpreting place names is fun, but can be problematic, and
Holderness is a case in point. It would be nice to err towards the
slightly romantic view that 'Holder' relates to the River Hull and
'ness' to a low island on a promontory jutting out into the sea, i.e.
the coastline and Spurn Point. However, it may also be that the
explanation lies, as suggested by Margaret Gelling and Ann Cole,
in Old Norse and Old English, with 'hērness', 'a district subject to
secular or ecclesiastical authority' (OE), and 'holdr', 'nobleman'
(ON). Yet as described by Thomas Blashill in 1900 the view to an
early settler who stood on the high ground of the Wolds and
looking east would be dominated by a great tidal inlet running
north from the Humber past what are now Beverley and Driffield,
and curving around towards the sea at Bridlington Bay. At times
of high tide and especially when the inland waters were in flood,
the Holderness coast would stand out like a great island cut off

from the mainland. Small islets would emerge from the expanse of grey mud, brackish and stagnant waters, green holmes in the midst of a vast waterland. To reach what Blashill describes as the Isle of Holderness, the naze or ness, would require either crossing the water by boat or else heading north and then east along the Wolds and across towards Bridlington, and then south along the coast.

Defoe's view related very much to the coastal zone and probably reflected the fact, of which he was most likely unaware, that centuries of aggressive coastal erosion had washed away towns, villages and presumably any great houses. The agricultural writer Henry Strickland presented a rather different view in 1812:

> Formerly, a clay soil was alone thought desirable for cultivation, and a low rich one for residence; the fuller of marshes, fens, and lakes, the better, as affording, probably, additional accommodations for rural life, and additional amusements, now held in little estimation. Hence, Holderness, Harthill, and Ouse and Derwent, were full of the seats of nobility and gentry: a century ago . . . they possessed not fewer than eighty-nine mansion-houses, and a century and a half before that sixty-eight, where there now remain only forty-nine! Whereas a change of opinion and manners have preserved to Buckrose and Dickering (upland countries) twenty-five, where, in the reign of Elizabeth, there were twenty-four.

This gives an insight into the perceived landscape and its uses and the impacts of fashions and the tastes of the nobility and landed gentry. Important to what follows is the desirability of wetlands and their associated features in the 1700s, but the change to more utilitarian functions by the 1800s. Interestingly the agricultural commentator William Marshall, born and living in North Yorkshire, never got as far as visiting Holderness. His one attempt to do so in the late 1700s was hindered by the weather: 'the extreme wetness of the autumn would have prevented me from visiting a low country, at that season'. This in itself is a testimony to the condition of the land. Marshall does provide some description of the landscape as viewed from the high ground of the Wolds with

> its surface broken into swells and hollows, but never descends to low land; the area of the district being free from marshes and fens. Towards the mouth of the Humber, some considerable extent of marsh lands occur, and in entering Holderness, from Hull, a flat of rich marshes, some two or three miles wide, are crossed; and between Hull and Beverly [sic], a considerable extent of fen lands lie a disgrace to the county; but not particularly to Holderness; whole lands rise out of the way of waters . . .

This gives a fair account of the situation with drainage and improvement which occurred during the later 1700s.

The Holderness wetlands were made up of the major valley of the Hull, and then the numerous meres and carrs, the last remaining being the largest, Hornsea Mere, and four smaller river valleys east of the Hull. There were also varying amounts of coastal salt marsh and flats. Marshland and carr woodland extended across the wide valleys to the foot of the Wolds, and a broad belt of salt marsh, natural and reclaimed, covered the southern area close by the Humber. The meandering rivers met the coastal tides

Curlew

and backed up to give a waterlogged whole with occasional islands raised out of the expansive waterscape. Almost all these areas have been removed and the history of this was described in two wonderful papers by June Sheppard (1958, 1966). Water-logged carrs occurred across the area, including the great Wallingfen, and huge amounts of water emanated from the powerful springs at the base of the chalk Wolds. The situation in Holderness is always complicated by the intensive coastal erosion of this seashore, and the shifting sands and flats along the northern shore of the Humber. Furthermore, the other major influence on the wetlands of the lower valleys is the conversion of the once extensive sheep walks of the Yorkshire Wolds to intensive farm-land. This has hugely influenced both the wildlife of the region and the hydrology of the wetlands. As noted by Sheppard, the East Riding of Yorkshire once held some of the most extensive tracts of marshland in England, with those of the Hull Valley extending north from the Humber for about twenty miles. They ran from Hull to Great Driffield with a lateral extent varying from around two to five miles. To the east was the clayland of Holderness with its glacial deposits of soft erodible boulder clay. West of the valley there is the higher ground of the Yorkshire Wolds chalk, from the bottom of which emerge powerful spring-lines. Islands of higher and drier ground stood out from the valley-bottom wetlands. This whole area was subjected to periodic and often severe flooding from water coming down the valleys or from tidal inundation from the south. There were scattered coastal settlements around the salt marshes along the Humber shore and along the Holderness coast, but most of these have long since been lost to the sea.

There were two main river valleys, the Hull and, to the east, the Old Fleet. The valleys had extensive peatlands and abundant freshwater marsh and fen. Water flooded from springs along the Wolds' edge and from the northern heads of the valleys. Typical of these valleys was that they have a very slight fall and so the streams and rivers meandered sluggishly through multiple braided channels and swampy vegetation. The water, unable to flow easily downstream, frequently spewed out of its channels and across the landscape. This periodic flooding of the valleys would vary in depth from just a few centimetres around the edges to perhaps two metres in the deeper areas; the whole fluctuating with the weather and the seasons. In the shallow flooded areas willows and alders were abundant, and the deeper waters probably remained year round as permanent meres. Accumulation of decaying vegetation created a deposit of peat varying from a metre to two metres or more. The more wooded sites were known as carrs and ultimately these were an intimate part of the landscape and later of the productive system of the region. Villages scattered around the drier ground on the edges of the floodland utilized the fens for fish, fowl, wood, grazing and other materials or products. The early communities would have used the rivers for transport and exploited the natural free resources of the valleys. The deeper peats in the carrs were exploited for peat fuel.

The resources of these wetlands could be important, as demonstrated by Humberstone's report of a survey of the Leconfield Estate for the Earl of Northumberland in 1570 (in Sheppard, 1958).

To the sayd manour also belongyth a great fenne, called the Carre, th'erle hath a great marke of swannes and also many wyld fowle, and a very profitable fishing which th'erles have always reserved to their owne possession for th'use and comodyte of their house, and appointed foure keepers or overseers, as well of the fowle as the fyshe, and every of them hath for his travayle or paynes about the same iiis. Iiijd [3s 4d]. And where as the tenauntes had comen of pasture in the same dry yeres, the dryft of the cattell dyd disturbe the bredying of the wyld fowle and especially of the wyld swannes, the late erle compounded with the tenaunts to forbere there comen in that fenne and payeth them yerely in recompence thereof xiijs. Iiijd [13s 4d].

Furthermore there were steps taken to enhance the value and benefit of for example the wildfowling with the construction of a number of duck decoys. These raised around ten per cent of the value in rental of the pasture but nevertheless were an important part of a mixed economy. These were undoubtedly productive lands and as such the uses and values are reflected in legal deeds. For example, a conveyance of Low Bransholm Farm in Sutton in Holderness to the Corporation of Hull in 1828 noted:

> All the lordship and manor of Sutton in Holderness with all the rights, royalties, members, and appurtenances to the same belonging or appertaining, wastes fishing places, hunting, hawking, fowling, turbary, suit sole, mulcture, free warren, mines, quarries, escheats, heriots, court leet and view of Frankpledge, perquisites and profits of courts and lets, and all that thereto appertaineth, goods and chattels of felons and fugitives, waifs and strays, deodands, villains with their sequels, fairs, markets, pie-powder courts, stallage, tolls and customs whatsoever to the said lordship and manor belonging or appertaining.

This document appears to be covering all bases whether or not the uses and rights really occurred and were active. However, it does give some insight into the complexity and potential value of the wider landscape resources.

The Beginnings of Improvement

In order to drain and improve these landscapes for farming, there is a need for co-ordination and organization. There may have been some modest impacts during the Roman occupation but the main efforts really began in medieval times and largely through the influence of ecclesiastical foundations. There were some limited enclosures and reclamations of coastal salt marshes by Danish and Saxon settlers, but this was always restricted to the easiest sites. Some large banks were built along the lower rivers to help protect areas from inundation by high tides, and the associated place names indicate that these were by Scandinavian settlers. It seems that the southern salt marshes were considered most useful and in many ways the easiest lands to reclaim and this was where the medieval improvers concentrated their efforts. Protective banks were built along the shores of the Humber and the Hull to hold back high spring tides. Drainage dikes were constructed by some local landowners and before 1200 the lords of the manors of Faxfleet, Blacktoft and Thornton Land had done this. Ecclesiastical holdings were especially forward thinking. Thirteenth-century documents for Holme-on-Spalding-Moor, for example, talk of marsh and woodland, and of dikes, assarts, ditches and enclosures. They also indicate new settlements such as Bursea and Hasholme founded on the reclaimed lands. It is known that the Humber shore banks were already constructed before the fourteenth century when King Edward II had commissioners repair and maintain them, work being noted in both 1311 and in 1313. These constructions were only of mud and turf, the easily and freely available local materials, and so exceptional tidal or storm events would breach them fairly easily. It was recorded by the Chronicle of the Abbey of Meaux that in 1265 the Humber floods reached as far as Cottingham. The commissioners of banks and sewers (drains) were appointed to address these problems. However, there was generally a problem that the commissioners were mostly active in the case of a problem or an emergency and there were serious issues of a lack of long-term maintenance.

Bridlington Priory was an active reclaimer of these lands in the villages where it had ownership. By the thirteenth century too, Meaux Abbey was in dispute over fisheries at Hornsea Mere, which remains today as the East Riding's largest water-body. Fisheries were important too at Wassand, Pidsea, where today the village name remains as a marker of the lost wetland, and Marr at Sutton. There was also an eel-pond at Brandesburton, the fishery of Eumerske at Burstwick, and meres at Skipsea, Lambwath, Withernsea and at other locations. All these have gone. There is further evidence of reclamation with Meaux Abbey taking in 400 acres at the appropriately named Moor for Moor Grange outside the town of Beeford. This was just one of several extensive ecclesiastical estates. The priory also had interests in the other productions from the marsh and fen landscapes. An Inquisition for Richard de Lascy for the Prior and convent of Bridlington in April 1300 stated that:

> It is not to the King's loss if he give leave to Richard de Lascy to grant pasture for 300 sheep in Folketon, and 50 cartloads of turves in the marsh [marisco] of the same Richard, to be dug and led away by the men of the prior and convent, and to the prior and convent of bridelingon. Held of John, baron of Craistok, by the service of 16s. a year for all service, the baron holding of Sir Robert de Tatissale, and roberrt of the King. Pasture worth 3s. a year. Each cartload of turves from the said marsh, to be dug and led at the costs of the prior and the convent, it is worth a penny.
>
> *Writ dated at Rokingham, 25 April 1300.*

These were complex and valuable productive landscapes.

There was a further complication too, in that the banks built to protect and reclaim valuable salt marsh also held back the waters flowing downstream and out to sea. In the pre-reclamation landscape this water had seeped away through a myriad of small creeks and channels across the salt marsh. To help alleviate this difficulty a series of ditches and drains was built to carry the freshwater away and with primitive sluice gates to stop the entry of sea water the other way. Within and around this landscape of farming improvement and land reclamation there emerged as series of small medieval settlements, encouraged no doubt by the perceived opportunities for gain. One of these communities was at Wyk [Wyke] and this became the property of the Crown under Edward I following a land-swap with the monks of Meaux Abbey in 1293. Edward renamed this township Kingston upon Hull. This was indeed rich pasture land but it came with problems of flooding and general inundation with constant care required for the flood banks and causeways built to allow transport across the marshes.

Hull has, and has always had, at significant threat of inundation from land and from sea. The abbey became a major landowner in the district and, fuelled by commercial exploitation of farmland in this productive landscape, they needed effective transportation. To achieve this, the monks constructed, as the Romans had before them in some fenlands, channels as both drains and canals. Some were cut anew and others were modified streams and rivers. The aim was to connect the productive farms to the River Hull and then the Humber to facilitate transport of goods out and to the markets. These canals included Eschedike (1160–1182), which joined the abbey to the River Hull, and Monkdike (1210–1220), which diverted water from the Lambwath (a tributary of the Old Fleet) and via the abbey grounds into Eschedike. Forthdike (1221–1235) ran between Wawne and Sutton to take the bulk of the remaining Lambwath flow. Skernedike (1210–1220) connected the river to an abbey grange to the north. Some of the early coastal reclamation was eased by the relative lowering of sea level around 1100 but by 1200 this was reversed and life became more difficult for the coastal dwellers. Both Meaux Abbey and Bridlington Priory were active in improving lands in the upper Hull Valley and reclaiming areas to meadow and pasture.

Whilst the canals certainly had a drainage impact, being five or six metres wide, their primary function was for transportation, to take produce from the abbey lands to the marketplace. The management of this landscape by the abbey was certainly more organized than that which preceded it. With economic interests in sheep and wool and other farm produce the monks worked the land and the waterscape reasonably efficiently. Fish and fowl would be important products and no doubt reeds, brushwood and peat fuel were also utilized. Although some of the river channels and the fenland was altered, the carrs and deeper meres would have been little changed. It appears that there was little new construction of drainage banks between 1300 and 1550, but the maintenance of existing ones was improved. There were attempts to relate the areas of land which benefited from each bank or drain and so to establish a basis for future taxation should it be necessary. When maintenance was specifically required, then Commissioners of Sewers were appointed to get the works done. By 1532 an act, The Statute of Sewers, was passed to provide organized Commissions of Sewers for all the main areas of fen and marsh across England and Wales. These commissions were appended by the Crown with standard procedures and powers to raise taxes and to undertake necessary works relating to drainage and flood protection. Raised from the local landowners and significant persons, they held Courts of Sewers and drew on the assistance of juries of twenty-four men in each hundred. These jurors were responsible for the inspection of the drains and banks and then deciding upon the onerous task of allocating responsibilities for maintenance.

These were significant undertakings and the Hull Valley, for example, had two such Courts of Sewers. The main court was held at Beverley, which covered the east of the East Riding and had beneath its jurisdiction smaller courts for the North, Middle and South Holderness, Hunsley Beacon, Bainton Beacon and Dickering. There was a separate smaller court for Hullshire, the administrative area for the south-west between Hull and the Wolds. The basic role of these courts was to ensure the maintenance of the system but not necessarily to improve upon it. Descriptions in the records leave little doubt as to the poor state of repairs over the period up to the mid-1600s. This was indeed the conclusion reached when a bad storm breached the Drypool Bank in 1646. Both banks and channels suffered from a lack of basic maintenance. There was limited new work to relieve flooding of the main road into Hull during the 1640s (under the instruction of the Privy Council), but beyond this very little was done.

However, in the early 1660s a very comprehensive survey and assessment was undertaken of the work of the Court of Sewers in the east part of the East Riding. This was no doubt spurred on by the great undertakings on the Bedford Level and before that at Hatfield Chase. There was a new spirit of improvement in the air, and changes would soon come to the Holderness fens. It was becoming clear that if these lands could be rid of their waters, then it would be possible to grow productive crops, or at least have good pasture. The publication of major books such as William Dugdale's *History of Imbanking and Drayning* in 1662 must have influenced the thoughts of all right-minded and forward-thinking landowners.

A Time of Improvement

The period from 1660 to around 1760 saw an upsurge in interest in the improvement and drainage of the carrs in the south-east of the Hull Valley. Separated from the reclaimed marshes of the Humber by a constructed bank, the water of the carrs further north was allowed to flow through a narrow gap in this bank, called Gold Dike Stock. Water drained this way all year round but particularly in winter. Clearly if the carr lands to the north of the bank were to be drained and improved, then this bottleneck would require attention. However, the people of Sutton, with their interests further downstream, objected most strongly to the ideas of widening the gap or keeping it open for longer periods. This illustrates very nicely one of the key problems of the drainage of lowland wetlands in flat landscapes: that of co-ordination and co-operation. However, a further drainage channel was cut and steps were taken to open the stock for longer and to keep it clear of debris.

By 1675 there were more ambitious plans drawn up to begin the drainage and improvement of the carrs, with the lead taken by Sir Joseph Ashe of the Manor of Wawne. His works changed and improved the drainage network and raised new banks to protect his land against inundation from elsewhere in the Hull Valley. He also brought a new technology to bear on the problem. He had two windmills built to lift water from his new Engine Drain and into the River Hull. This meant that the drains could be cut deep into the carrs and the water could be lowered effectively, as long as the winds blew. As the peats dried and shrank and the land surface dropped, so more windmills were constructed to carry the water off. In many ways this was the beginning of the end for the Holderness Carrs. Other landowners quickly followed suit and the drainage windmills or 'engines' were commented on by the agricultural improver Arthur Young when he visited the Holderness area in the late 1700s. Sheppard (1958) suggested there were maybe eight or so drainage engines in operation in the south-eastern Hull Valley in the early 1800s. Away from Hull and closer to the headwaters with their powerful springs the job of drainage became more intractable, but the process had begun and in a century or so would have run its course.

The Holderness Marshes and Carrs in the 1700s and 1800s

A survey by John Grundy in December 1763 suggested a depth of water in the eastern area of between two feet six inches and four feet eight inches. Sheppard (1958) suggested that the water across the north and west was probably deeper still. In 1743 Thomas Browne surveyed the Brandesburton area for the City of London, describing Great Ox Carr (an area of forty-nine acres) as 'coarse boggy land in which no cattle can go it is in a Dry Year always mown and the Sedge and Flaggs serve for young or dry cattle in the winter but this is under water 9 months at least and sometimes all year.' Nearby Ing Carr covered 556 acres and this included some higher ground more suitable for grazing stock. However, this was described thus: 'Above three parts of it is nothing but boggs upon which no cattle ever goes and in a wett summer at least 9 parts in 10 lyes under water and the gates or Commons are then not worth 2d a piece, but such summers as the three last they have been let from 2s 6d to 4s. The surface of the water upon Hull River is higher than four fifths of this Common.' The problems of water levels and the consequent difficulties in effecting drainage are very apparent from this description. Yet the carrs had value within the local economy and were used for summer cattle grazing. Other land was thus released to be used for meadow or arable and the cattle could then feed on the aftermath after cutting or mowing. The cash value of the carrs for rental was considerably less than the other, drier lands, but they were important in the overall system. In a wet summer when cattle could not go on to the carrs then there would be other associated problems.

Beyond this the carrs were the best local source for peat fuel, provided brushwood and perhaps small timber, and would also be good for certain fish species and for wildfowl. Peasant cottagers and smaller farmers, both having common rights, would value the pasture for their livestock very highly. They also took reeds for thatching and probably sedge and flagg too. The lands released from constant flood by the windmills would be turned to both pasture but especially arable, and an important crop was rape seed. This provided colza oil for lamps.

The southern silt marshes were still highly valued and generally maintained free of flooding. In his itinerary, John Leland had noted this area as 'very fruteful of medow and pasture'. But in 1646 there was a calamity when a great storm burst through the Drypool Banks. The small settlement of Stoneferry was 'drowned by the force of ye waters for the time of 26 weeks and the inhabitants of Stoneferry, Sudcoates and Marfleet were enforced eyther to leave their houses or betake themselves to their Chambers and putt forth their goods to other places, and many of their goods were drowned to their great loss and damage.' And he continues, 'for a longe time all people both horse and foot inhabiting that part of Holderness were deprived of going to any market but with boates' (quoted in Sheppard, 1958). Life in and around the waterscapes was often fruitful but frequently difficult and perilous.

The difficulties and disasters helped to focus efforts on long-term solutions, and the opportunities for financial gain from land improvement increasingly grabbed the attention of landowners. With drainage it was possible to improve summer pasture and in some cases to grow arable crops too. In the area north of Hull the main landowners got together to fund a scheme to drain the carrs as far as Brandesburton and Burshill, and the engineer John Grundy was commissioned to draw up a plan. Having obtained the necessary Act of Parliament, the project fell by the wayside due to wrangling about compensation over the Wawne area and opposition from shipping interests in Hull. Scouring of rivers and estuaries to remove silt deposition was often vital to the viability of coastal harbours and ports, and the diversion of large amounts of freshwater to new channels threatened their livelihoods. Some of the Grundy plan was implemented but with only one quite small new drain. The rest was left pretty much as before. Maps of the time show a number of meres still existing in the Leven and Tickton Carrs and therefore little evidence of any permanent lowering of the waters. Some improvement was apparent, however, and this was enough to encourage landowners to put through a joint enclosure and drainage act for the area in 1766. This spurred on a scheme that improved mixed peat and silt marshland around Cottingham. The project was followed by the Beverley and Skidby Drainage Act in 1785 with a new cut taking water direct to Hull. An act of 1792 addressed the lowlands of Hessle and Anlaby, south-west of Beverley. The combined impact of these localized initiatives was eventually to separate the major flooding areas of the northern carrs from the Humber shoreline to the south.

Again we see the conflicts and issues which tended to dog attempts at coherent co-ordinated actions. The continued existence of the intransigent flooded areas of the northern carrs actually helped the southern zone, since they absorbed much of the floodwaters which spilled out across the wide upper valleys. When the northern landowners began to sit up and take notice of improvements further south, it was seen that their own drainage efforts might cause problems in the southern area. The Holderness Drainage Trustees through the Court of Sewers stipulated constraints on what might be done. This included for example a directive that any banks on the west side of the River Hull must be at least 150 yards back from the riverbank to allow floodwater capacity, and that 300 yards of such banks must be at least 6 inches lower than the lowest 100 yards of the Holderness banks.

During the late 1700s, the debates continued as to how best to effect the drainage of the remaining carrs. Various solutions were proposed, including new cuts to the south, but again falling foul of the shipping merchants of Hull. In 1798 the Beverley and Barmston Drainage Act was passed and the waters which previously drained from the northern carrs south to Hull were diverted by a new cut to the sea at Barmston. The impact was considerable since this was a large, straight cut taking lowland water direct to the sea. Floods did continue and there were also complications with inland navigation and the demands of the Driffield Navigation Canal, the lock for which contributed to further flooding upstream. Parts of the level were still flooded in winter and occasionally in summer, such as in July 1828 when the drainage surveyor 'sailed in a boat, without much interruption, over land and fences, in a direct line from Hull Bridge to Frodingham Bridge'. Despite the problems and the risks, by the early 1800s the carrs in the Beverley and Barmston level were mostly under the plough and growing oats, barley and wheat. Just the lowest land now remained a permanent pasture.

However, by the late 1700s a problem had become apparent as had happened on a grand scale in Cambridgeshire. As the drainage took effect, the peat shrank and the land surface subsided. This took large areas of land down below the cuts that were supposed to drain them. Pumping by wind and then by steam would begin to assume more importance. Two other changes happened over this period: a downturn in agriculture in the early 1800s and at the same time the expansion of Hull into a modern and thriving port. The former meant a decline in conditions as drains fell into disrepair but the latter removed the need to scour the old Hull harbour-mouth. As Victorian agriculture boomed the landowners gained an Act of Parliament in 1832 to take a new drain into the Humber at Marfleet. This actually passed in a culvert underneath the older upland drain. With this innovation and other associated changes, the meres of Leven and Tickton disappeared from the map and flooding diminished. By 1868 steam pumps were being used but there were still complicated interactions between land drainage and navigation, which meant some flooding still occurred. The dredging of the River Hull between the Old Harbour and the Driffield Navigation finally went ahead after 1880, along with the raising of the riverbanks. Together with steam pumps at Arram Beck, Hempholme and Dunswell, these improvements finally put an end to the flooding of the Beverley and Barmston Level. However, the picture was not the same across the whole area and the Holderness Level still experienced some problems. Thomas Blashill, writing of Sutton in Holderness in 1900, noted that:

> Notwithstanding all that had been done to protect the low lands in the parish from floods, the North and East Carrs were, within living memory, still liable to be flooded, and in one case at least a voyage was performed from Fairholm to Sutton village in a boat. About the year 1835, a new drain was cut, under an Act of the 2nd William IV., through the Carrs to take the low-land waters to a new outlet at Marfleet, and if this has not entirely remedied the mischief, it has left an occasional reminder of the far-off time when the Carrs were marshes, and the lowest portion of them was occupied by Sutton Marr.

Interestingly, whilst pumping was hugely successful in getting the floodwaters away, changes in land use were exacerbating the difficulties. With the introduction of tile drains to farming improvement this innovation had been taken up across the Holderness area. The consequence was that this took rainwater off the land very quickly and instead of being held back the water added to peak flows of floodwater and overtopped the main drains. A similar problem occurs in the same areas today. Furthermore, the increasing areas of land under cultivation and wrested from the 'waste' by the improvers would have dramatically increased this effect. Parliamentary Enclosures affected huge areas: 68,000 acres in Holderness and 206,000 acres on the Yorkshire Wolds. The solution to this final problem was enhanced pumping to take water off very efficiently just west of Marfleet, and the consequence was a dramatic reduction in flood risk.

The Final Stages

Allison (1976) quotes an observer in the Yorkshire Wolds describing the landscape on view:

> The country is all enclosed, generally by thorn hedges; and plantations, everywhere grouped over its surface, add beauty to the outline, while they shelter the fields from cutting blasts of winter and spring. Green pasture fields are occasionally intermixed with corn, or more frequently surround the spacious and comfortable homestead. Large and numerous corn ricks give and air of warmth and plenty, while the turnip fields, crowed with sheep, make up a cheerful and animated picture.

By the late 1800s the bulk of the waterscape of Holderness had gone and the farmland around it or which replaced it was also intensively drained and under-drained. At the same time the upland sheep walks of the Wolds were mostly enclosed and improved and this entire landscape was transformed to what it is

Great Bustard

today. The twentieth century continued the process with agricultural subsidies from the UK government and then the EU, with massive simplification of the farming landscape and technological and chemically driven improvement. The old lands and the waterscapes remain in name only and in the hidden topographical detail of the region. The fens, marshes, swamps, carrs and meres together with their meandering sluggish rivers have long gone, to be replaced by structured, controlled and efficient farming. Prosperous farms of consolidated enclosure holdings of the 1700s and 1800s are dotted across the land with rigid lines of enclosure quickthorn hedges and drains. This modern landscape would be almost unrecognizable to a visitor from the early 1700s!

Chapter Four

York and the Vale of York

West of the high ground of the Yorkshire Wolds lies the expansive, generally flat and for much of its history poorly drained Vale of York. Most of the marsh ground was located to the southern end, close by the Rivers Ouse and Humber. However, along the length of the meandering Rivers Ouse and Derwent there were carrs, peat bogs and other wetland areas. The lower reaches merged into a salt marsh around four miles wide, subject to regular tidal inundation. North of this marsh were the extensive carrs and marshes, of which the largest was the great Wallingfen that covered the flatlands as far as Holme-on-Spalding-Moor and Market Weighton. This area was fed by water from both the river floodlands to the west and from the River Foulney, which carried spring water from the foot of the chalk Wolds.

One of the Vale's great rivers was the Yorkshire Derwent, which rose from the North York Moors and entered the Vale of York at Stamford Bridge, to be joined further down by the Pocklington Beck. Across this landscape the only truly dry areas were the raised islands such as Holme-on-Spalding-Moor, Newton and Wheldrake. Both sandy and clay areas were largely inundated throughout much of the year.

York was long established as a major centre not only in the north and Northumbria, but in England too. However, the city has always been vulnerable to flooding, and is sat between major rivers and extensive marshes and bogs. The Vale of York, now famous for its rich farmland in early medieval times, was still extensively wooded and often wet with expansive marshes and swamps. Woodland extended from the River Ouse in the west to beyond the Derwent in the east. This was woodland not like our woods of today, but extensive grazed wood pasture, and much became royal hunting forest and remained under Forest Law until 1235. Large areas of this extensive forest and wood pasture remained into late medieval times with individual woods extending up to 500 acres or more. Today the most extensive wetland is the river valley washland at Wheldrake Ings National Nature Reserve, and it was around here that under royal licence early taking-in or assarting of the forest to farmland was occurring around 1235. Once Forest Law was removed from the area, then the process of improvement and enclosure could begin in earnest. So by 1300 the woods and moors of Wheldrake were being reduced by conversion to arable land by local villagers, some used in common and some by individuals.

The Vale of York is mostly flat, but in parts has an undulating surface of boulder clay. It had numerous meres and carrs, abundant streams and extensive marshes. This low-lying and

Gathering leeches in Yorkshire

mostly poorly drained landscape was not conducive for extensive open-field arable farming, and much remained as unimproved commons, waste or marsh. Some of these commons such as Skipwith still had extensive scrubby woodland as well as areas of carr and deep peats. In sandy areas such as east of Holme-on-Spalding-Moor, the commons were extensive areas of heath and furze. The most extensive area of such waste was that extending north from Broomfleet by the Humber, north towards Holme and Market Weighton. Holme Moor covered 7,000 acres and Wallingfen around 5,000 acres. Across the southern expanse of the Vale were numerous other commons many hundreds of acres in area. In the northern part of the Vale were extensive commons around Tillmire, the medieval peat cut for York, and which spread across Heslington, Fulford, Deighton, Wheldrake, Dunnington and Elvington. Further south was waste shared by Skipwith, Riccall, Osgodby, Cliffe and North and South Duffield. In the 1600s some of the sandy commons were used for rabbit warrening, as happened on an industrial scale in the Wolds.

Drainage Comes at Last

As was the case in Holderness, the earliest attempts at reclamation and drainage were at the southern end of the Vale, and were targeted at the extensive salt marshes along the Humber shore. In the post-Conquest period, the Bishop of Durham was the Lord of Howdenshire and led the process of embankment, protection and drainage. The reclaimed areas needed both banks to the north to protect them from freshwater flooding and, associated with this, drainage dikes cut through the reclaimed land to carry the freshwater off. These drains, such as Thornton Dam, Temple Dam and Hansard, were cut from the Foulney to carry water south to the Ouse. The lanes which ran parallel to them are still reflected in today's landscape with the modern roads. Before these drains were cut the Wallingfen area was described as for the most part resembling a lake. Following the imposition of these drains there was seasonal lowering of the waters to allow summer use for cattle grazing.

As early as 1300 the drainage around Wallingfen facilitated the use of its carrs for peat cutting for fuel and for summer pasture for livestock. By the early 1400s the fen was cut in two by the Langdike, a straightening of the Foulney, and this was reflected in the accounts of the Wallingfen Court from 1425 onwards. Up to the early 1600s the responsibility for drainage and protection from flooding was shared across the Vale and across Holderness, and it seems that the latter took precedence. However, from 1676 responsibility for the drainage of lands in the Vale of York was separated from that for the Holderness area, but again progress was slow certainly before 1730. As in nearby Holderness the main progress, described above, was with coastal reclamation along the Humber shoreline. During the 1700s and 1800s the long drawn out process of drainage and improvement removed the wetlands and replaced them with new, ordered and productive farmland. The result here, as across much of Holderness, was a distinctive landscape described by Allison (1976) as 'bleak . . . windswept expanses of reclaimed land, a landscape planned to the smallest detail and unrelieved by any relict features of an older more natural countryside'. In 1540 Leland had noted areas of Howdenshire that he had seen as being hedged and given over to pasture, though there would have been arable as well. Elsewhere, such as at Wressle, he described how 'This Ryvver at greate Raynes ragith and overflowith much of the Ground there aboute being low Medowes.' His view might well reflect the ease of access to the parts that he witnessed. Even in the 1720s Defoe still described much of the area as given over to floods, and stated that 'The Derwent is a River very much full of Water, and overflows its Banks and all the Neighbouring Meadows, always after rain.'

Some work was done to deepen stream channels and to straighten watercourses, but generally the Vale still experienced widespread flooding with associated loss of crops and livestock. The winter floods could be devastating but the rich, silt-laden floodwaters brought nutrient-rich silts and so the summer meadows were highly valued by local villagers. However, there was always the threat of summer floods, which could damage or destroy the valuable hay crops. During the medieval period some attempts were made to build protective banks along parts of the Derwent to protect the summer meadows from excessive damage. With an emphasis on livestock, especially cattle, in the local economy, grassland was very important. With summer meadows requiring the exclusion of stock, the animals would be pastured on more recently improved lands close by. The end came quite quickly. Bishopsoil, with 4,000 acres of poor clay soils and peats, had been left unimproved due to both the poverty of its un-productive soils and the threat of floodwaters. The area was also subject to winter floods because the drains that it shared with improved lands elsewhere, and which lowered the water sufficient for summer pasture, were blocked in winter to allow the other lands to remain dry. This meant that Bishopsoil was waterlogged for much of the winter. It was enclosed by Act of Parliament in 1767 with two major drains to take off the water and discharge to the Ouse. The land so reclaimed would provide valuable summer pasture for cattle. As late as the 1700s Wallingfen included several permanent meres, the largest being Oxmardike Marr and Yapley Marr. Other areas were temporary seasonal flooded carrs covered by water for between three and ten months of each year, but their 5,000 acres were drained and enclosed in 1781. The carrs north of Langdike had provided important summer pasture for the villages of Holme-on-Spalding-Moor, Cliffe, Hotham and others. Interestingly the records of the Wallingfen Court, which controlled the uses of the common, have been preserved. This set down the number of animals the commoners could put out and this was, in 1591, fixed in relation to the number of animals for which an indi-vidual farm could provide winter fodder. The controls helped prevent cattle from other areas being brought to Wallingfen for summer pasturing. Further rules were added, such as in 1636 that nobody could pasture more than 160 sheep on the common at any time, or their equivalent in horses or cattle, with 1 cow equalling 5 sheep, and 1 horse 7. As pointed out by June Sheppard in 1966, with 850 to 900 people holding common rights, even with this limit there could in theory have been up to 70,000 sheep and 13,000 cattle. Since this is around five times the carrying capacity of the best pastures today, it is assumed that numbers were in reality much lower. Within the Vale the carrs were economically very important. Along with the grazing they also provided grass, sedge and other herbage cut from the wetter areas and taken for winter fodder. Gorse and other scrub on drier ground provided firewood, peat turf could be cut, but only the 'surface spit', and there were fish and wildfowl too.

Parliamentary Enclosures affected 45,000 acres in the Vale of York and the last areas to go were quite late, in 1904, near Skipwith. The Vale still suffered serious flooding especially around the valleys of the River Derwent and the Pocklington Beck. By the twentieth century the Beck was dredged and embanked to further reduce the risk, though even today the floods have not totally receded.

Landowners began to focus on the potential to improve the agriculture of the Vale of York round about the mid-eighteenth century. The move towards this end had three main objectives based around the drainage of lands within the Vale and the reduction in associated flood damage, the enclosure and improvement of commons and wastes, and finally the improvement in communications and transport. This last consideration was very important since it would connect the area's improved agricultural production to the potential markets, and it could mean a compromise between drainage and provision of canal-based transport. One of the first landowners to lead this new enthusiasm for improvement was Mr Leuyns Boldero. In 1748 he acquired the estate of South Cave and the associated interest in Wallingfen, and by 1772 there was an Act of Parliament to promote the work. The Market Weighton Navigation and Drainage Act addressed both drainage and the necessity for effective transport. Not all the proposals were implemented and the costs of those which were undertaken were apportioned between private investments in the canal scheme and a tax on the owners of low grounds affected by flooding. The new canal was cut between 1772 and 1782. Water was carried off quite quickly, but more so from the higher, northern carrs than the southern fen. In the northern carrs with the water dropped, the surface peat was burnt and oats could be grown for several years. The southern areas were still too wet to plough, but although the overall improvements were less than had been hoped for, it was enough to encourage further interest and to weaken the centuries-old common usage. The Market Weighton Drainage Commissioners enclosed 490 acres of Wallingfen Common on either side of the canal in lieu of taxes due for the drainage works, the lands remaining exempt from drainage taxes until 1938. Under the 1777 Wallingfen Enclosure Act the rest of the area was enclosed although the complex divisions of rights amongst neighbouring villagers took time to resolve. Most of the northern part of the fen was enclosed by 1780.

It seems that across Howdenshire and the once vast Wallingfen, the 1700s saw effective drainage and enclosure and a conversion of wetland to productive agriculture. This was not the case across the whole of the Vale of York, and other areas remained less improved. In 1794 Isaac Leatham stated that 'There is no want of water in this division, in many places it lies too near the surface.' One issue was the significance of the Rivers Derwent and Foulney and the level of water in the Market Weighton Canal, which made it difficult to lower the water-table in the surrounding land. Localized improvements were brought about by the deepening of field drains and the use of deep ploughing to facilitate drainage, but an overall scheme was not forthcoming. During the 1800s relatively little further activity happened since agricultural drainage would disadvantage the canal and that was of greater commercial value. This waterway carried agricultural produce to the markets, but also carried coal and lime to the urban areas, and bricks and tiles now manufactured alongside its banks. In 1840 over two million bricks and tiles were being transported. This was the situation prevailing in 1831 when the Surveyor of the Beverley and Barmston Drainage noted that he could distinguish three grades of land in the area of the old Wallingfen. He described these as 'some . . . constantly flooded, others are so in particularly wet seasons, and others although never flooded are so much saturated with water as to render them unproductive'.

A key change in this situation was the advent of the railways and therefore the national demise or at least drastic reduction in commercial worth of the canals. With decline in the upkeep of the canal and simultaneously a reduction in the importance of its brickworks, the possibility was there for a renewed interest in wider drainage in the Vale. There was even a move in the early 1900s to close the canal navigation and devote it totally to drainage. However, the remaining brick makers objected and a compromise was reached. This situation still limited the potential for drainage and this situation was exacerbated by the downturn in the agricultural economy in the early part of the twentieth century. The Market Weighton Drainage Board was established in the 1930s but this area still remained the least improved of the old marshland areas and a rich haven for wildlife species. In the valley of the River Derwent the drainage also deteriorated during the latter part of the nineteenth century. The Court of Sewers for the west parts of the East Riding had gone into abeyance in 1843, and the York to Malton railway had opened in 1845. The consequence was that the navigation interests in the river declined and with it the clearance of weeds and sandbanks. As the vegetation and sand accumulated the river increasingly burst its banks out on to its floodplain. In fact the flooding became more frequent and prolonged than anything since the early medieval period. With the formation in the 1930s of the Lower Derwent Internal Drainage Board the inexorable move towards improvement grew once more. The riverbeds of the Derwent and the Pocklington Beck were dredged and cleared and the Yorkshire Ouse River Board built new flood banks along the river close to its confluence with the Ouse. Other minor drains and adjacent watercourses were cleared, deepened and where necessary straightened. This work addressed many of the problems but some flooding and waterlogging continued and indeed still do. Because of the intractable nature of the great wetlands of the Vale of York and the Derwent Valley, a few areas still retain more than a hint of their medieval landscape. These are now mostly recognized and important conservation sites and indeed a part of the bigger picture today of adapting to climate change and alleviating flood risk elsewhere. The valley bottom marshlands are important washlands, vital for winter flood control of the River Derwent, and important as a part of the agricultural economy and landscape.

Chapter Five

The Vale and Lake of Pickering

17,500 acres, lying on the banks of the Rye and Derwent, in the
North and East Ridings of this county, are either greatly
damaged, or rendered entirely useless, by the overflowings
of those rivers.

John Tuke (1800)

An Introduction to Lake Pickering and its History

Sandwiched between the Yorkshire Wolds to the south and the
high massif of the North Yorkshire Moors to the north is the most
northerly of the Yorkshire fenlands, some 17,500 acres of marsh,
fens and sedges. This is the broad swathe of the former prehistoric
Lake Pickering, an area of low-lying and mostly flat land with the
deep solid geology of the Kimmeridge Clays (Lower Jurassic clay
beds) on which sit glacial boulder clay, sands and gravels, and alluvium and peat. This great lakeland environment gradually infilled
and dried through natural processes, but much of the wetland
survived as open water and as marsh or fen into the historic period.
It has been shown that Lake Pickering was an extensive proglacial
lake of the Devensian glacial period, filling the Vale of Pickering
between the North York Moors and the Yorkshire Wolds. This was
when ice sheets extending from Scandinavia blocked the drainage
of the area. Water had previously flowed north-eastwards past
where Filey is today and towards the basin of what is now the
northern North Sea.

It is believed that north of Lake Pickering the North Sea ice sheet was held back by the high ground of the North York Moors. The Cleveland Hills diverted British ice from the north to the west of the Vale of Pickering and down the Ouse valley. The northern valleys of the North York Moors had small inter-linked proglacial lakes in the head of Newton Dale, the area which now leads south to Pickering. The North Sea ice sheet blocked the earlier drainage outlet for the Vale of Pickering, which then filled and overflowed between the Howardian Hills and the Yorkshire Wolds. The drainage flowed south into the much larger proglacial lakes (Lake Fenland and Lake Humber) which filled the lower valley of the River Ouse, of the River Trent, and through a narrow gap at Lincoln and into the Fenland basin. With climate change over long periods the extent of ice in the Ouse Valley fluctuated with two significant terminal moraines, at Escrick and at York. The lake waters rose to the point where they overflowed southwards to cut an outfall between the Howardian Hills and the Yorkshire

Throxenby Mere from an Old Postcard

Wolds. This was near to today's Kirkham Priory between Malton and Stamford Bridge, to create Yorkshire's River Derwent. The outfall of water flowed between the ice and the Wolds to the north arm of Lake Humber and then Lake Fenland. At Kirkham, the junction between Lake Pickering and the southern lakes was narrow but variable over time. The early surface of Lake Pickering was higher than that of Lake Fenland to the south, but the two water-bodies eventually became parts of a single functioning wetland.

In the modern period the River Derwent, draining a large part of the North York Moors, has been modified with an artificial flood relief channel which diverts water from the river about ten kilometres above West Ayton, prior to reaching the flatlands of the Vale of Pickering. The water flows east along a new channel, the Sea Cut, through what was formerly a dry valley formed from a possible peri-glacial overflow channel. It then passes into the course of the Scalby Beck through Scalby and on to the North Sea.

The Vale is well known from prehistoric settlements in and around the wetland areas and these provide an insight into the landscape and also to the people who lived there. The most famous archaeology site is Star Carr. This internationally significant Mesolithic site is located about five miles south of Scarborough. Occupied from around 8770 BC until about 8460 BC, the evidence belongs to the early Mesolithic Maglemosian culture that was present across the Northern European lowlands. There was probably a period of abandonment between 8680 BC and 8580 BC perhaps due to climate change and related impacts on the lake water levels. Star Carr was discovered in 1947 by John Moore, a local man from Scarborough, whilst clearing a field drain. Excavation by Professor Grahame Clark of Cambridge University of 1949–1951 found what he described as a 'brushwood platform' on the edge of the former Lake Pickering. It is likely that the platform was laid down to help consolidate boggy land around the water's edge. There have been a number of programmes of archaeological excavation and research that have provided real insights into the lives of early settlers in these wetlands across the whole region. The studies revealed people living on the dry land above the lake and around the lake edge, and perhaps seasonally. Research indicated the various activities these people undertook, perhaps hunting animals such as red deer, roe deer, elk, aurochs and wild boar. It is likely that activities and prey varied with the seasons and over the several hundred years of its occupation. As in many ancient wetlands that survive today, the lake sediments preserve evidence of the past, such as primitive tools and other items dropped into it. At Star Cross these include artefacts like the hunters' tools, such as flint scrapers used to clean animal skins and work bone and antler. The sources of flint, hugely important to this culture, came both from nearby coastal beaches and from the Yorkshire Wolds. One find was a fragment of a wooden oar, which confirmed that these communities used boats, most likely coracles or dugout canoes. This would be important for travelling to hunt and fish, to move between settlement sites, or perhaps to trade. The islands which stood out above the lake waters also have evidence of occupation and the boats would facilitate movement between these and the shoreline. Other artefacts found here include ornamental beads of stone and amber, which suggest personal adornment and also trade routes over longer distances. Archaeologists have also discovered the remains of domesticated dogs. One find from here was of headdresses made from red deer skulls complete with antlers, possibly used as a disguise during hunting or maybe in ritual or story-telling.

The Wetlands of the Vale of Pickering

Today the broad Vale of Pickering, watered by the Rivers Derwent, Rye and their tributaries, contrast with the higher country which surrounds it. Here there are level pastures with grazing cattle and arable fields; a flat, rich farming landscape. When John Leland, the Royal Antiquary of Henry VIII, came to Pickering he described the country between Scarborough and Pickering as by hille and dale meate plentifull of corn and grasse but litle wood in sight. The toune of Pykering is large but not welle compact to gither. The greatest part of it with the paroch chirch and the castel is on the south est part of the broke renning thorough the toune, and standith on a great slaty hille. The other part of the toun is not so bigge as this: the brook rennith bytwixt them.

Royal interest in the area goes back further and Henry I granted Archbishop Gerard of York 'soc and sac and all customs and freedom from all customs in his lands in Pickering'. The Dean of York held a carucate of land in Pickering as a rectory manor, and an ancient demesne of the Crown. This had attached to it 'house-bote, haybote and nuts as estovers'. Furthermore, the deans were 'quit of payment for herbage and pannage, lawing of dogs and puture in Pickering Forest'. They also held a three-week court for their tenants and had amendment of the assize of bread and ale. Nearby Marishes with the low-lying land north of the River Derwent were refered to in Domesday (1086) as Odulfesmare, Chiluesmares, Aschilesmares, Maxudesmares and Chigogemers; all good wetland names. These formed part of what was known in the twelfth century as 'the Waste by Pickering'. Henry II then gave the waste with its common of fishery in the Rivers Derwent, Costa and Rye and all the demesne waters of the forest to Rievaulx Abbey; a grant later confirmed by both Richard I and King John. During the reign of Henry II a number of landowners disclaimed their rights to the lands in the waste and associated uses in favour of the abbey. These included Stephen Mangevilein, Roger de Clere, William de Mandevill Earl of Essex, and William de Forz Earl of Albemarl.

Henry II gave Rievaulx a further two carucates of land called Kilverdmersh or Chiluesmares, and Robert de Roos waived his claims on Theockemarais and Loftmarais to the abbey. This gives an impression of a very wet but nevertheless valuable landscape across the Vale, unenclosed and yet productive.

William Marshall in 1796 described the Vale of Pickering as

William Marshall

having a larger diameter of about thirty-five miles and its greatest width of about twelve miles 'including, in its area, and the cultivated lands which hang upon its banks, and which as property belongs to it, about three hundred square miles, or 200,000 acres'. Its topography was extremely flat and almost level but with scattered hillocks across it and with promontories intruding into it from the marginal banks. The Rivers Derwent and Rye he describes as rising in 'moreland mountains' and winding through wooded valleys and into the flatness of the Vale 'through which they move with sluggard pace, to their narrow outlet'. He suggests that

> As proof of the flatness of the Vale, the waters of the Rye are some four or five days, in passing from Hemsley to Malton (about fourteen miles): and those of the Derwent, not less than a week, in moving from Ayton (about fifteen miles) to the same outlet.

He goes on to suggest that

> It is highly probable that, in a state of nature, a principal part
> of the Vale was subject to be overflowed. Even now, since
> rivers have been cut, and embankments made, extensive
> fields of water are still to be seen, in times of flood; not,
> however, through natural necessity, but for want of further
> exertions of art.

However, despite this natural propensity for flooding, Marshall
felt that 'By increasing embankments, and by removing obstruc-
tions natural and artificial, the rivers, in their highest swell, might
be kept within due bounds.' Later in his account Marshall details
how the river embankments should be raised at about ten, twenty
or thirty yards from the riverbank itself in order to allow volume
into which the floodwaters can spill. As he states 'their rise will be
proportionately less, and the requisite height of bank will of course
be lessened, in the same proportion'. He also suggests that this
approach has the additional benefit of depositing floodwater silts
on the land between the embankments and so filling in any
remaining marshy ground and effectively raising the whole area.
The constructed embankments also provided 'places of safety, for
stock to fly to, in floods; a species of refuge they had not, when the
whole lay open'. So although the lands enclosed by riverside
embankments might be viewed as waste ground by landowners,
Marshall argued they provided benefits other than just flood
protection. Fertilized and productive due to silt deposition they
were good pasture and could also be adapted as osier beds for
basketry.

Marshall (1796) also noted good examples already undertaken
in the Vale, such as Brawby Moor,

> containing about three hundred acres of low marshland soil,
> over run, in an open state, with furze and rushes, together
> with some interspaces of sedgey grass, was liable to be over-
> flowed by the river Severn, which runs on the upper side of

it; the Rye, which washes it on the other side, being its natural shore.

The Moor was owned by the Earl of Salisbury and was enclosed by about three-quarters of a mile of embankment at a cost of £60 or 1s per yard. The bank was around seven feet high and sufficiently wide on top to allow cattle to walk on it. The enclosure, the road and associated buildings cost about £300 in total but the rental value was increased by around 100 per cent in year one but with an expected rise of at least 400 per cent after ten years of further improvements undertaken by the tenants. Here we see the clear financial incentive for an individual landowner to embank the river and to improve his or her land. Marshall also explains how the commoners had also implemented a partial embankment of the river through the mechanism of an act of enclosure and had 'widely secured the lower grounds to be enclosed, from the waters of floods, which have, hitherto, occasionally overflowed them.' In this case the embankments were considerably lower, just two to three feet. The land value was raised by 200–300 per cent. In essence, Marshall advocated 'Converting the lower lands to arable, inclosing the commons, and laying the arable fields to grass' to bring about as considerable change 'in what may be called the ECONOMY OF LIVE STOCK'. The result was to move the farming of the Vale into a state of productive agriculture from the original condition where 'In the uninclosed state of this Vale, the Commons and Cars were applied, chiefly, to the rearing of WORKING OXEN, and a few DAIRY COWS.' John Tuke followed Marshall as an advocate of such improvement. Writing in 1800 he provides the following account of this district:

> Ryedale, with the East and West Marishes, form one vale, Pickering beck dividing Ryedale from the Marishes . . . The surface of the lower parts of Ryedale is flat, and a large proportion of it, probably not less than 7,000 acres, liable to be flooded, the waters being much retarded by the extreme curvature of the river, and kept up by a mill of little value at

Newsham, and still more by those at Malton, which raises the water ten feet and four inches. The bridge at Kirby Misperton also contributes much to keep up the floods; it has only one arch, which is quite insufficient for admitting the sudden torrents which rush from the moors after heavy rains; an additional arch might be built at a very moderate expence. In general, the Rye, as well as the smaller streams falling into it, have been embanked, but almost always injudiciously, not upon any regular plan, and without leaving sufficient fore-shore; the consequence has therefore been, that by contracting the passage for the water, the force, rapidity, and height of the stream have been greatly augmented, the probability of the banks breaking increased, and when broken, of doing additional injury, particularly in the summer time; and, where both sides of the river have not been embanked, of throwing with increased power an accumulated weight of water on the opposite shore.

Along with the suggestion of the modifications to bridges and to mills, Tuke advocated the cleaning out of the riverbed and setting sluices to take off the excess or waste water from the mills at Old Malton and at New Malton. He further proposed floodgates at Newsham Mill and various other engineering interventions. It was these ideas and their implementation which ultimately tamed the Vale's natural tendency to wetness and flooding. For a fuller understanding of the processes and the changes which followed it is necessary to place water and its management into a broader context of landscape history.

Water and Landscape History

For a thorough overview of the landscape history of the North Yorkshire region the book edited by Robin Butlin (2003's *Historical Atlas of North Yorkshire*) provides an ideal account, and the contribution by Noel Menuge covers the Vale of Pickering specifically.

Today's landscape is dominated by agriculture with arable in the east and pastoral farming in the west. However, the valley's prehistory was dominated by water and significant wetland remained until relatively recently. Evidence of early water-bodies includes settlements like Star Carr both in and around the former lake and on its islands. The Roman roads and other trackways through the area had ditches along either side to help their drainage in a clearly very wet environment. The first significant documentary evidence comes from the Domesday account (1086) which provides place names associated with wetlands: Chilusmares, Aschilmares, Maxudesmares and Odulfsmere (within Marishes in the central part of the valley), Loft Marishes and Ghigomersc (in Thornton-le-Dale). These names with 'marishes', 'mersc', 'mere' and 'mares' all imply wetlands. There was also a considerable amount of land noted as 'waste' and this was probably wet and difficult to cultivate, but often suitable for grazing livestock. Other settlements were described as having 'meadows', which again may be a typical wetland fringe use for productive land not capable of being ploughed.

As noted for other parts of the great Yorkshire wetlands the main early efforts directed at land improvement and drainage were untaken by the monasteries and associated religious houses. So by the high and late Middle Ages it was indeed the monasteries that controlled the cultivation and drainage or other improvements in the Vale. By 1301, in the central Vale alone, there were eleven monastic marshland granges: Loftmarsh (Rievaulx), Kekmarsh (Rievaulx), Lund (Rievaulx), Newhouse, South Marton, Edston (Malton Priory), Ryton (Malton Priory), Selleybrigg, Kirby Misperton (Malton Priory), Rook Barugh and Normanby. Other granges farmed around the edges and on the drier gravel or limestone areas, and with their arable land these were worth more. However, the gradual process of improvement was taking place and some ploughing for arable was possible, such as at Kekmarsh where in 1274 there were 300 acres under the plough with a similar area in pastoral use. It seems that Rievaulx Abbey dominated land management in the central part of the Vale of Pickering and

Yedingham Abbey held lands in the west with carrs, marsh and lakes. Along with the religious houses there were other individual landowners and their peasants, but it was the monasteries that led on co-ordinated attempts to drain and improve. Only they were able to apply the necessary resources and to generate from such investment the financial incentives to undertake major works. So until the break-up of the great religious houses and their estates this was the main human force at work to tame nature. As in the other examples described in this book, the changes in climate with the colder wetter influences of the so-called Little Ice Age and the limited technologies available to shift water from the land did little to help their cause.

The Drainage

In 1800 John Tuke was able to write that:

> In a country of so various a surface as is that of the district under survey, there is ample room for draining of every description. It is here, as elsewhere, found, that of all operations in husbandry, none pays equal interest for the capital bestowed upon it; none has a greater or more immediate effect; none so surely repays both landlord and tenant.

He continues in the same vein to state that:

> Sufficient attention, however, has not yet been here paid to the great features of this improvement; neither to that of draining off the flood-waters, and excluding them from the lands, by opening out and clearing the rivers, and by judicious embankments; or of carrying off the rain, or surface-waters and upper springs, by means of under-drains.

Tuke focused on the problems of Rye Dale and the Vale of Pickering where he says:

Upon the Rye, and its branches, various embankments have
been made but never on a judicious or scientific plan; too
contracted a space for the water has always been left, by
which its force has been augmented, and weak banks
rendered still less able to resist its violence; and no attention
has ever been paid to straightening the course, and clearing
out the bed of the stream. For want of similar attention,
considerable tracts of land are injured on other rivers; but in
no instance to be compared with the damage suffered on the
Rye and the Derwent.

This was a view at the start of the nineteenth century but it
reflected the problems of nearly three hundred years of inaction.

With the dissolution of the monasteries and the establishment of
Courts of Sewers by King Henry VIII, there was clearly some
continued effort to control waters and to cultivate the land.
However, with the loss of the economic power and organization of
the monasteries and the changing and generally deteriorating
climatic conditions this was no doubt problematic. It seems that
there was relatively limited active drainage in the Vale during this
late medieval and post-medieval period and certainly writers such
as Leland around the early 1500s refer to extensive wetland and as
late as the 1780s the Pickering farmer William Marshall noted that
the Vale was mostly in 'a state of fenn'. Indeed, Marshall in 1787
described the situation as 'A disgrace to the country.' At this time
there were floods along the whole length of the Rivers Derwent
and Hertford, and it was calculated that because of the meandering
rivers it took around a week for the water to travel the fifteen miles
of the Vale.

The agricultural writers of the later period in the 1700s and
1800s, such as William Marshall, Arthur Young and John Tuke,
were strong advocates of 'improvement' and their views on the
Vale of Pickering were from this standpoint. Marshall suggested
that the River Derwent ought to be 'banked out' and that the area
should then have a series of key drains and ditches established to
take water off and to prevent flooding. Tuke in 1800 concurred

with this opinion and local landowners realized that this was land which if drained could be good agricultural farmland. The resulting drainage schemes of the nineteenth century did exactly this. The major landowners – the Cayleys of Brompton, Humphery Osbaldeston of Hunmanby, the Ledgerds of Ganton, Lord Derwent of Hackness and Lord Downe of Wykham – arranged to meet and discuss the problems and issues. As a result they commissioned a Mr Milburn to survey the land between Malton and Hackness and from this to propose to suggest a suitable drainage scheme. In 1779, following serious flooding of the Vale, an Act of Parliament was presented in order to drain the area. The focus of the drainage works began with this Parliamentary Act passed in 1800 and affected the eastern Vale settlements of Muston, Yedingham and Wykeham. The project was based on proposals outlined on a map of the Vale by William Chapman (who had responsibility for Scarborough Harbour Docks). The Muston and Yedingham Drainage Authority was then established in order to undertake the scheme. The Derwent was straightened and largely embanked, the Hertford was engineered to become an embanked straight drainage channel, and the sea cut was dug at Scalby to take excess water off and directly to the North Sea. This canal is still present and also called the Scarborough Sea Cut or the North Back Drain.

The resulting drainage with the enhanced power of Victorian engineering, co-ordinated finance and the possibilities of steam and wind power quickly removed the standing water and lowered the overall water-table across the Vale. These major agricultural improvements benefited townships across the area, notably Flixton, Staxton, Folkton, Seamer, Ebberston and Willerby. So the aspirations and frustrations of John Tuke had been effectively addressed. When he wrote in 1800 that 'The drainage of this tract has been several times in agitation; but a contrariety of interests, and injudicious mode of setting about the business or the want of the active abilities of some individuals, has hitherto put a stop to it; and the undertaking seems at present dormant' he would have found it hard to imagine the removal of almost the entire wetland by 1900. H Rider Haggard, when writing of agriculture in Yorkshire in 1902, makes no mention of the floods or the waters here. A further incentive to improvement was provided by food shortages during the Napoleonic Wars and the consequent high prices of grain. A similar effect was felt in land improvement and drainage during the two World Wars of the twentieth century.

More Recent Times

The remaining wetlands or at least 'wetter' lands are now highly regarded for conservation of both nature and heritage; receiving funding and protected status as a consequence. Yet despite the efforts of people over several centuries the problems of water management in this most northerly of the Yorkshire Fens have not totally gone away. As seen elsewhere the agricultural depression of the late 1800s meant a lack of maintenance of the ninety-three bridges, of drainage structures and sluices, and of the eighty miles or so of rivers in the drainage district. Similar problems threatened in the 1920s and Catchment Boards were set up under the 1930

Boating on Mere at Scarborough

Land Drainage Act with powers to carry out improvements and maintenance to so-called Main Rivers and to supervise and encourage internal drainage boards.

However, in 1947, despite these efforts, disaster struck with catastrophic floods affecting Malton and Norton. A consequence of this impact was a programme of improved engineering works implemented over the period up to 1970. Sluices were constructed at Kirkham Weir, and the channel through Malton upstream to Yedingham was engineered. The old Yedingham Bridge, a severe barrier to effective drainage, was eventually replaced by the new bridge and associated deepening of the river channel by around one-and-a-half metres. Other works included channel straightening and the construction of other new bridges. In tandem with all this activity efforts were made to encourage good and effective drainage of agricultural land in the surrounding districts. Of course, an obvious impact of this sort of 'improvement' is to shift water rapidly downstream rather than retaining it in the catchment, thus exacerbating any flood risk in the lower reaches. In the period from 1970 until the present day that is exactly what has happened, and the floods continue.

Chapter Six

Draining and Improving Yorksire's Fens

Science and Landscape

> The soil of the isle of Axholm, is among the finest in England;
> they have black sandy loams; they have warp lands; they have
> brown sands; and they have rich black loams, soapy and
> tenacious; the under stratum at Haxey, Belton etc. is, in many
> places, an imperfect plaster stone.
>
> *Arthur Young (1772)*

In England the drainage of fen and swamp in the 1600s was closely
followed by the English Civil War; later these same landscapes
bred the Methodists and the Quakers. It may even have been the
experiences of Royalists returning to their estates from exile in
the Low Countries that was a pivotal moment in the changed
approach to productive landscapes. They came back often poor
(relatively) but with ideas of land improvement from Holland,
Flanders and France that they wished to implement on their own
estates. An example of this was the case of Heneage Finch, Third
Earl of Winchilsea, in the East Riding of Yorkshire. Saddled with
debts due to his part in the Royalist rising of 1655, from 1657–1658
he travelled in Europe. Whilst abroad he began to formulate and
draw up plans for the improvements to his estates that would be
necessary on his return, the objective being improved farming and

increased rents. In particular he focused on his 'low lands'. The approach was to be deepening of the beck and of ditches and more draining of the extensive wet areas. His accounts demonstrate the exchange of ideas and techniques and also the pre-eminence that the Cambridgeshire fens achieved in terms of their reputation, or at least that of their improvers. He offered to pay for a man:

> to see the late great drains of the Fens of Lincolnshire and the Level of Bedford, Isle of Ely and others thereabouts, and any other works you think necessary, and to take observations, and draughts of all such works and engines, as may be of use to our land, he may likewise endeavour to procure such workmen and tenants as may be most advantageous to my . . . drowned lands.

The intention was to remove water using pumps such as a portable horse-mill, and with ditching and banking to at least piece-by-piece improve and drain the floodlands of his estate. The idea of

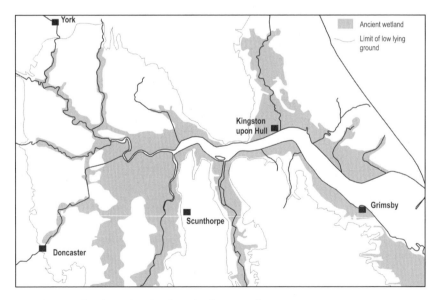

Humber Wetlands and Vale of York after Van de Noort

mills to pump water off the carrs was from Holland. Once drained, the land would be enclosed and farms built on it, stocked with cattle and carts and riding horses. Trees (alders and osiers, with 10,000 willows a year) were to be planted. These would provide shade in summer, shelter in winter, and timber to burn or sell. Better pasture land held in common was to be ploughed and arable areas to be enclosed. There was little suggestion that there might be opposition to this, of if there were that it would pose any problem. Thus we see the ideas of European scientific farming being imported into England. Not that the ideas translated into immediate action. The East Riding carrs of Winchilsea's estates were not finally drained until the nineteenth century.

Tensions often grew between old, established rural communities and incomers over colonization and improvement. This was certainly the case in the English fens, when European settlers arrived on their doorstep to drain their wetlands. Co-operative work between the two groups occurred around the boundaries of established fields and the edge of common waste, but problems arose over important common rights. In marginal landscapes common and traditionally held rights were hugely important. The titles of particular types of occupiers clearly differentiated their status. Later, when commons and wastes were under threat of enclosure and 'improvement', those without established common rights had nothing. With population increase and rigorous controls over common usage, there were issues of ownership and protections for commoners already in place, and competition between neighbouring settlements.

The relationship between agriculture and its natural resources and the progress of industrial development is critical. Industry and urbanization require increased agricultural productivity, allowing the primary sector to meet the rise in demand for food. Important too is the ability of farming to 'release' resources (mostly labour, capital and land) to support industry and services. To do this, agricultural revolution must go hand in hand with industrial revolution, and maybe political revolution. Such changes might include new techniques and equipment to cultivate the soil, new ways to drain and 'improve' land, advanced crop rotations, heavier stocking of animals and intensification of mixed husbandry. The processes included increased productivity on land already farmed and extension of the agriculture into new long-since-abandoned areas. After around 1840 there was also the option of increased artificial chemical fertilizers and rapidly evolving farm machinery. Additionally, the ways that land was held, owned or managed changed with enclosures and consolidation of farm holdings, all closely inter-related. An influx of European settlers changed the face and even the culture of our fens. People and skills associated with both farming in the wet landscape, but especially in helping to drain it, were eagerly sought by landowners. All across Europe the skilled peasants, many from the Dutch, Flemish and French wetlands, migrated and settled in areas such as the fens where landowners and others welcomed their services.

The famous but controversial Dutchman Cornelius Vermuyden moved to England to take on a series of major land reclamation projects. The first big one was the draining of Hatfield Chase, south of the Humber Estuary, from 1626 to 1629. He also advanced projects for similar massive draining of the Somerset Levels, although these were never executed. As Marc Bloch has suggested, these Dutch engineers did not undertake this work purely for the public good: their operations in the fens and also in the French coastal marshes were proto-capitalist exercises 'directed by an association of technical experts and business men . . . financed by a few large business-houses, mostly Dutch'. Their objective was less public land reclamation than private wealth generation. As such, these wetland initiatives became the financial models for further eighteenth-century reclamation enterprises in Brittany and Guienne, where 'companies were founded for the express purpose of financing – or indeed speculating in – land reclamation, which now also received government patronage'. Obviously, as noted earlier, there was often deep suspicion, indeed open hostility, among local land workers towards these speculators and investors, these 'adventurers' as they were sneeringly called by the seventeenth-century fenmen who smashed their sluices and pulled down their dikes. The idea was germinating that not only were foreigners being employed to take away the English fens, but that it was paid for by foreign money. This not only caused resentment but a deep suspicion about where it might end, especially for the fenmen when Dutch and Flemish settlers moved in 'next door'.

Nonetheless, financial greed was not in itself a great enough incentive to drive the early modern processes of wetland draining, clearance and cultivation. Exploiting the general reputation of marshes and bogs as places of evil and infamy, religion and public morality were also invoked as reasons for their reclamation. Indeed, the very notion of 'reclamation' – as with the later eighteenth-century idea of 'improvement' – struck a strong moral chord with contemporaries, especially among the first generation of engineers and drainage experts in England, many of whom were Protestants and Huguenots fleeing religious persecution and civil strife on the continent. Effective draining, then, was crucial, and it involved both the removal of water from the landscape and the protection of areas by embankments. However, the situation is more complicated since removal of water might be by simple gravitational drainage, but often there was a need to pump the water to a higher level. Here technology became a limiting factor. By 1710, the English reclaimers of the fens had imported from Holland the technique of using windmill-powered pumps to drain the wetlands. But this alone was not enough to facilitate widespread cultivation of the land, because the effective drainage of field soils was also necessary, but still not fully understood. It was not until much later in the century that a further discovery and subsequent innovation in draining expanded the practice of wetland reclamation, first in Britain and then on the Continent. This took place near Leamington Spa in 1764 when a local farmer, Joseph Elkington, solved the problem of under-drainage, of clearing not just the surface waters from an area of wetland but of siphoning off low-level underground water tables by tapping and diverting their springs. In 1795 the British Parliament awarded Elkington the handsome sum of £1,000 in recognition of his innovation and asked him to survey the general application of his method of under-drainage in other parts of the country.

Increased food production was also a major incentive for fenland drainage in England in the eighteenth century. Arthur Young, writing in 1772, suggested 'breaking up uncultivated lands' and 'draining fens' as the chief means not only of enhancing productivity of these holdings but also of raising income for those who farmed them. The logic was straightforward: reclaimed lands could be enclosed and incorporated into the new crop rotation cycles, which avoided leaving fields fallow. They could specifically be used for cultivating fodder crops which in turn would feed greater numbers of livestock which would, in their turn, produce more manure, further reducing the need for fallow and fertilizing yet greater yields on the reclaimed lands.

Dutch, French and Flemish Connections in Yorkshire's Fens

Over the whole period from 1600 to the 1800s there was extensive interchange of ideas about land improvement between Britain and continental Europe. This became more than an exchange of ideas (as happened in metal-working when experts came from Germany to establish industries in England) when land improvers were hired from the Low Countries. The most famous was Dutch drainage engineer Sir Cornelius Vermuyden, along with Dutch, Flemish and French skilled labourers. To drain Hatfield Level of the Humber, the drainers employed French, Flemish and Dutch workers. Many locals opposed importation of labour and skills. Willing and skilled workers were provided by French Protestant Huguenots and Low Country Walloons fleeing Catholic persecution in the sixteenth and seventeenth centuries. Many of these refugees were glad to be in Protestant England, both groups were French speaking, and the Walloons in particular were knowledgeable in land reclamation. They were in three main occupational groups, two being workers skilled in land drainage and farming.

Both influenced subsequent approaches to England's lowland fen areas.

The Fenland Drainage

To understand the process of drainage and reclamation or 'improvement' of the fenland landscapes and waterscapes, it is necessary to bear in mind the fluctuation levels of land and sea over the time period and the changing human pressures, aspirations and applications of technology. To effectively drain land in a flat, expansive landscape requires knowledge of water and land management, but also suitable engineering technology to undertake and maintain the process. In part, therefore, drainage follows the evolution and availability of necessary pumping, dyking and draining technologies. However, in a flat land you also need political control and co-operation so that everyone drains. To drain one area but not another cannot succeed. In this way much of the lowland fen differs from the wet land on hills and higher ground, where very often a single parcel of wet land can be effectively drained by an individual owner. Finally, though, the process has to be driven along by an economic or other social pressure. There must be capital available and a financial incentive to undertake considerable work and to maintain the system once it is in place. This all takes place against a long period of time and a backdrop of rising and falling sea levels and therefore of increased and decreased risks of massive and catastrophic inundations. The position of the land–sea interface varies with changing levels and as material is dumped by the rivers converging through the fens and into the Wash. Local people on the one hand benefit from the unfettered use of the wetland resources and therefore resist enclosure and drainage. On the other hand, in a waterscape, they live with the constant risk of major flooding, and may therefore support some degree of embanking and flood risk management.

The Early Drainage

As in the East Anglian Fens the first attempts at co-ordinated drainage of the Yorkshire Fens began with the Romans. Constructing causeways and canals, they sought to both control and to utilize the extensive wetland landscapes. Although many canals and drains undoubtedly had a land improvement function, they were also very important for transportation. This might be of produce and animals, or of soldiers and military equipment. There is still some debate as to the origin of the Turnbridge Dike, the River Don's northward channel in the Humberhead Levels, perhaps a major Roman military canal. Van de Noort argues that this may have been a pre-existing river channel present certainly in the late Neolithic and early Bronze Age, perhaps straightened and improved by the Romans. The Bycarrs Dike that links the Rivers Idle and the Trent in the south, and the lower parts of the River Derwent in the north, are also suggested to be Roman modifications. Along with the major structures there were extensive areas of coastal reclamation and innumerable small-scale drainage and restoration schemes around the fringes of the great Yorkshire fenland.

By the Middle Ages, with post-Roman abandonment and the impacts of fluctuating sea levels, the main drainage works were undertaken by the ecclesiastical centres with their extensive agricultural estates. These may have begun under Christian Saxon influences but interrupted by the Viking settlements, to be picked up once more after the Norman Conquest. As already discussed the abbey at Selby led the way in the north with major drainage schemes around Thorne Moors. The Abbots may have also undertaken some modifications to the Turnbridge Dike, though this is uncertain. Both ecclesiastical centres and nobility were involved in drainage schemes. Hugh de Pudsey was both Lord of Howdenshire and Bishop of Durham, and was responsible for the re-colonization of wetlands in the Vale of York. The Knights Templar at Faxfleet were involved in major water management works with the Temple Dam, and the Canons Thornton at

Thornton Land with the Thornton Dam, and Gilbert Hansard at Blacktoft with the Hansardam. Around the 1160s the Abbot at Meaux Abbey commissioned the construction of the Ashdyke in the lower Hull Valley. Primarily for transportation, this had a dual function of drainage with probably a network of lesser dikes across the area. North of Hull there was the construction of the Foredyke and possibly a complex of fishponds and a fish-house, all part of the Meaux Abbey estate. In the 1200s there were the first co-ordinated attempts to resolve issues of flooding in the Ancholme Valley with the straightening of the river between Bishopsbridge and the Humber. As in other parts of the region the silting of the river channels was always a problem and dredging was being undertaken from the 1300s onwards. *The History and Antiquities of Thorne* (Anon., 1820) states that: 'As early as the first of Edward III (1327) the inhabitants commenced the drainage, to improve the land and general face of the country.'

Colonizing and reclaiming the Yorkshire fenlands was always potentially problematic and many attempts failed. This was especially so when climate and sea level were changing so as to make life more difficult with poor crops and rising water-tables. There were further complications such as population decline due to the Black Death in the 1300s, and also changing economic and social circumstances. Much arable land was converted to sheep farming for the flourishing wool trade, but then labour shortages also made this difficult and people began a move into the urban areas. With cooler and wetter weather in the period from around 1250 to the late 1400s, and significant sea level rise, water was becoming even more of a problem. The Chronicle of Meaux Abbey reported extensive flooding in the Hull Valley during 1253 and 1265. Commissioners were appointed to assess the riverbanks and the sea defences in 1285 and there were continuing difficulties during the 1300s and 1400s. Some areas had new walls or banks built to provide defence in times of flood, and in other areas special ledges were constructed for cattle if the floods rose too high. It is clear that in these times of changing water levels the difficulties for those living in or around the Yorkshire Fens were enormous. In some cases lands were enclosed and defended, but in many situations there was abandonment and the farmers moved into the local towns. One consequence that was particularly important for the future drainage of much of the area was that the social, economic and political power over these lands ended up, for the most part, vested in just a few large estates. Following the dissolution of the monasteries lands were distributed to a few large aristocratic estates and the Crown.

The First Large-scale Drainage

During the mid-1300s Hatfield Chase was returned as property of the Crown, as a royal hunting forest under the jurisdiction of the Forest Law, an area reserved for the royal hunt and associated pleasures. However, by the time of the 1608 survey of the royal forests and chases, it was considered 'utterly wasted'. This is strange when the excellent hunting provided for the visit of Prince Henry is considered. It seems again that the perspective of the beholder may influence the judgment that is made. In 1600, under Elizabeth I, Parliament had passed 'An act for the recovery and inning of drowned and surrounded grounds and the draining dry of watery marshes, fens, bogs, moors and other grounds of like nature', intended primarily for the East Anglian Fens but applied first to the Yorkshire Fen and specifically to the area around Hatfield Chase. The passing of this act ultimately spelt the end for many wetlands. Fresh from the Low Countries, Cornelius Vermuyden was asked about undertaking the work. This phase of the drainage impacted on around 24,280 hectares of wetland in Hatfield Chase, Wroot and Finningley, the Isle of Axholme, and along the River Idle. The intention was to reclaim large areas of land and so render them suitable for agriculture. From the project only the present-day areas of Thorne and Hatfield Moors remained intact in the core zone of the Humberhead Levels and beyond this the more outlying wetlands in the constituent river valleys, along with the larger carrs such as Potteric, remained reasonably intact but in an increasingly dry landscape.

On inspecting the area and the task, Vermuyden declared the reclamation to be quite practicable. After centuries of local inability to remove the 70,000 acres of waters from the area, the people of the region were not convinced that it was feasible. After all, every previous attempt had literally floundered. The then king, James I, summoned a local jury to consider the issue and the task, but they broke up after stating that it was impossible. Vermuyden was prepared to take on the work and bound himself to achieve what the jury had stated could not be done. However, before he could decide what to do, James died and was replaced on the throne by King Charles I. He was familiar with the ongoing negotiations and confirmed the necessary agreements. On 24 May 1626 articles that had been drawn up were signed by Vermuyden and for the Crown. Vermuyden was contracted to reclaim the drowned lands and make them fit for tillage and pasturage. For this, he and his fellow adventurers would received one third of the reclaimed area. He went back to Amsterdam to raise the necessary capital and no doubt to recruit specialist skills needed for the undertaking. A company was then formed almost entirely composed of Dutch investors and the work began. They also brought over with them a considerable number of Dutch and Flemish workers. This at once bypassed the difficulty of recruiting local labour from communities opposed to the undertaking, and it also meant a workforce experienced in living in and indeed draining great wetlands. Some were already here, having been recruited to help drain Dagenham and Canvey Island on the Thames, and others because they were fleeing religious persecution. These included French Protestant Huguenots from Picardy and Walloons from Flanders.

The plan for the drainage operations was fairly straightforward. The Idle was to be diverted by straight channels into the Trent, taking out the meandering watercourse across the levels of Hatfield Chase. Deep cuts took the water from the main lakes and meres on the level. The River Don was to be taken north and prevented from entering the level by means of embankments, then directed through the Turnbridge Dike into the Aire. This was problematic because the channel was too small for the water to be carried and the result was flooding of the 'old lands' around Fishlake, Sykehouse and Snaith. The remedy, undertaken after Vermuyden had left, was to cut a new deep channel called 'The Dutch River' to take the water directly to the Ouse near Goole. The solution worked but at an enormous extra cost and to the detriment of many of the adventurers. There were also problems with the local people in this northern part of the area. They resented the project and also the workers who were brought in to do the job. They were decried as foreigners and marauders and, dissatisfied with the efforts of the Crown, they took the law into their own hands. They rioted and broke down the embankments and assaulted the Flemish workers; several people died in the conflicts and legal disputes ran for years. Often not recognized was the fact that Vermuyden did attempt to satisfy some of the grievances of the locals. Clearly the main issue was the loss of their lands and traditional rights, and there was nothing he could do whilst at the same time undertaking the work as commissioned. However, a further trouble was the employment of 'foreigners' to do the deed, adding insult to injury. To try to encourage a more positive attitude Vermuyden did employ large numbers of native workmen and he paid them considerably above what they were used to. Apparently he also tried to alleviate the obvious suffering of those adversely affected by the scheme. R Ansbie [Sir Ralph Hansby] wrote to the Duke of Buckingham from nearby Tickhill Castle in 1628:

What has happened betwixt Mr. Vermuyden's friends and workmen and the people of Axholme these inclosed will give a taste. Great riots have been committed by the people, and a man killed by the Dutch party, the killing of whom is conceived to be murder in all who gave direction for them to go armed that day. These outrages will produce good effects. They will procure conformity in the people, and enforce

Vermuyden to sue for favour at the Duke's hands, if not for himself, for divers of his friends, especially for Mr. Saines, a Dutchman, who has an adventure of 13,000 l. in this work. Upon examination of the rest of Vermuyden's people, thinks it will appear that he gave them orders to go armed.

According to Dugdale the works did reduce unemployment locally and where the country about had been 'full of wandering beggars' these had all disappeared. There was good employment at high wages for all willing to work. The reclaimed land, freed of waters, was to be made into valuable agricultural holdings, but this would require further long-term cultivation. On 6 January 1629 Vermuyden received a knighthood from Charles I in 'recognition of the skill and energy that he had displayed in adding so large a tract to the cultivable lands of England'. He also took a grant from the Crown of all the 24,500 acres of land reclaimed in the manor of Hatfield, at a rent to the Crown of £193-3s-5½d annually, one red rose ancient rent, an improved rent of £425 from Christmas 1630, and a cash sum of £16,080. He was also granted permission to erect one or more chapels for the Dutch and Flemish settlers to worship in their own languages. They also proceeded to build houses, farmsteads and windmills with the clear intention of long-term settlement of the lands recently won from the waters. For the locals though this was all serious provocation and caused major and continuing bitterness. They took issues into their own hands and obstructed the work on the drainage scheme. On 10 April 1629 a complaint was laid before the council board at Whitehall by the Attorney General and by Vermuyden with regard to the riotous behaviour of Robert Portington Esq and others in beating, wounding and killing workmen employed in the undertaking and 'for spoiling the walls made for the draining of the lands'. It was Roger Portington who had entertained Prince Henry. He had removed to the manor hall at Hatfield having received an inheritance from Sir Roger Portington of Leeds. *The History of Thorne* suggests that they were not actually related but that Sir Roger's widow left the estate to Roger Portington of Tudworth because he was her former husband's name double. Having moved to Hatfield Manor Portington lived there until the outbreak of the Civil War, at which point he joined the king's army as a captain. He spent £9,000 to raise and maintain his own troop, was taken prisoner and held for eleven years and had to pay £1,890 costs to retain his estate. Roger's brother Robert was a major in Sir William Savill's regiment involved in plundering the Isle of Axholme, but described as a valiant soldier. He too was captured and then imprisoned, this time in Hull. However, in dealing with the complaints of Vermuyden, Robert Portington and his accomplices were bound over, though he was allowed to continue as a Justice of the Peace, 'so long as he behaveth himself well'.

It is likely that the Portingtons were long established in the region with keen interests in the chase and the hunt, and they would not have appreciated the imposition of Vermuyden on their patch. His efforts were clearly detrimental to their enjoyment and possibly to their livelihoods. Yet there is a further twist in this tale, since when Roger Portington entertained Prince Henry to such wonderful hunting, one of the other guests of the party was . . . Cornelius Vermuyden. Indeed this was when he first conceived the idea of draining the Hatfield Chase and surrounding areas. If Henry had lived to be king, with his passion for the hunt it is unlikely that the undertaking would have come about. However, Henry died, Charles succeeded, and Vermuyden drained. The problems of violence by locals to the imported drainers and of new flooding to old lands by the malfunctioning drainage project were to rumble on for many years. The matter was taken to the Privy Council with complaints of lost rights and damage done to the surrounding districts by the drainage works. This resulted in an inquest held by the Earls of Clare and Newcastle and Sir Gervase Clifton. As might be expected, the hearing went in favour of Vermuyden. He had already subpoenaed many of original inhabitants for damages done to him and his agents, and several were apprehended and taken to York Gaol. The bitterness of the locals to the Dutch intruders grew stronger and the situation continued to deteriorate. Eventually Lord Wentworth, the President of the North, intervened and determined that the legal suits should cease. He also directed Vermuyden to assign to the locals certain tracts of moor and marsh to be enjoyed by them in common. Finally, after unsuccessfully disputing the directive, Vermuyden withdrew altogether from the adventure. He first put his interests in the hands of trustees and then pulled out completely.

After Vermuyden left the area the damage caused by the scheme to the 'old lands' was relieved at great expense by the cutting of the Dutch River, though there were serious difficulties in raising the necessary capital for the works. With all the problems that had ensued, the value of the adventurers' shares had plummeted. However, money was raised and the new river was cut, thus alleviating the serious cause of complaints in the north of the area. There followed a period of relative calm during which the settlers, dispersed across the reclaimed lands in individual houses, set about cultivating the land. However, the tranquillity was not to last, because promoted in part by the attempts to drain the Cambridgeshire Fens to the south, the English Civil War broke out. With the Yorkshire Royalists very active across the River Don, the Parliamentary Committee based in Lincoln watched over the region. It seemed that Sir Ralph Humby was about to march into the Isle of Axholme with a small force, and so to prevent this the order was given to breach the dikes and to raise the sluice gates at Snow Sewer and Millerton Sluice. The result was catastrophic inundation across the region that undid the drainage and cultivation efforts of many years. This was estimated to have caused damage to the settlers of around £20,000 in just one night. The local activists went further, wreaking revenge on those who had dispossessed them. The settlers' houses were wrecked, corn in the fields was destroyed and fences were torn down. When the settlers resisted they were forced at gunpoint to watch the area re-flooded, the rioters swearing that they would see the levels drowned again and the foreigners swim away like ducks.

Following the floods, the commoners set about claims as participants in the lands that remained dry and which were now free of the Dutch settlers. Colonel Lilburne, in charge of a force of

Parliamentarian troops, took occupation of Sandtoft, apparently driving out the local Protestant vicar and stabling horses in his chapel. The Colonel struck a bargain with the commoners that assigned 2,000 acres of Epworth Common to him personally, in exchange for recognition that the remainder were assigned to them. It was also agreed that he would uphold the claims of the commoners and prevent any redress by the now deposed settlers in terms of any claims to their own losses from the recent events. Despite Lilburne's influence and doggedness, the former settlers did get a ruling in their favour some eleven years after the event. The form of the settlement, however, prevented any major compensation, but some were able to return to their former dwellings and holdings. For years after the legal settlement the commoners continued at war with the settlers, both sides taking legal action and not averse to brute force too. A Mr Reading was engaged to defend the rights of the participants and settlers, but the commoners still resisted and tried to burn him and his family in their home. It was said that Mr Reading lived to a hundred years of age, but he spent fifty of those years fighting battles with the fenmen. He reckoned to have been involved in 'thirty-one set battles' with the commoners in defence of the drainers and the adventurers.

The lands reclaimed by the adventurers or participants were divided three ways with one third going to the Crown, another to the adventurers and Vermuyden, and the final one to the tenants, mostly local villagers with common rights. Financial backing for the scheme came from investors – 'participants' – many of who were landowners and financiers from Holland and France with previous experience of the economic gains from speculating in wetland improvement. However, apart from the problems of drainage itself there were major issues of challenges to the legality of the process from the commoners and other peasants, and acts of physical violence against the people and property involved in the undertaking. Much of the work was done by imported labour from Holland, France and Flanders; a skilled force with good knowledge of wetland drainage but very unpopular with the indigenous

locals. As a result of the unrest a Crown Commission was established to look into the grievances and the legal processes ran for
many years. The main dispute was the loss of common lands and
associated rights and the breaches of previous commitments to
maintain these in perpetuity. The complaints related to basic losses
of rights but also the impacts on the valuable floodlands no longer
fertilized by the annual dumping of mineral-rich sediments.
Arable lands that had formerly been dry were now wet due to the
changed hydrology across the region. The locals also lost major
sources of both sustenance and income through the decline of
fowling and fishing. On completion of the project the responsibility for its maintenance lay with the participants.

The principal mechanism for the drainage scheme was the
cutting of a new channel to take the River Don northwards to
the Turnbridge Dike and the Went, and then at a later date the
cutting of the Dutch River to take the combined flow of the Don
and the Went eastwards to the Ouse. This took away the south-
ward flow of the Don that formerly ran into Thorne Mere and
south then east to the Idle and across the south of Thorne Moors.
In the south of the area the River Idle was blocked at Idle Stop and
partially diverted into the existing Byker's Dike, but also down the
newly cut New Idle, and the Double Rivers to the River Trent. The
River Torne was also diverted north-east through a new cut,
the New River Torne, and passed under the New Idle at Tunnel
Pits. The scheme also involved a general straightening and deepening of rivers and other channels. During the Civil War the
commoners sided with Parliament and continued to sabotage
the drainage works. They also attacked the settlement of the
imported drainage participants who had sided with the king. After
the war finished the Parliamentarians continued the drainage
begun by Charles and the legal disputes and occasional acts of
violence or sabotage continued.

As in the East Anglian Fens a fundamental problem with
draining these peatlands was that once dry they shrank and so
ended up lower that the drains. In the north this necessitated the
cutting of the Dutch River to alleviate problems of flooding

the reclaimed land. Vermuyden however, perhaps sensibly, had already sold his interests in the scheme and moved on, leaving the mopping up to the other participants.

As with many of the major drainage schemes of the time, the problems were not immediately solved and breaches in the flood defences, accidental or deliberate, caused disaster and damage. Further manipulation of the original project was needed for the next 200 years as further cuts were dug and new innovations to drainage and pumping were applied. The Mother Drain was constructed in the south between 1769 and 1803, to take water from Everton, Gringley and Misterton Carrs. It was here at Misterton Sluice that the first steam-powered pumps were installed and so began the final phase of human dominance over an intransigent nature. Engineering works continued throughout the period and in 1862, as specified in the original agreement signed by Charles I, the Participations were incorporated by Act of Parliament.

The Progress of 'Improvement'

No doubt whilst Vermuyden wasted away in penury and the commoners mourned their losses, others must have gained considerably from his activities in both north Lincolnshire and South Yorkshire, and in south Lincolnshire and Cambridgeshire. Yet the drainage of the fens was by no means complete, although the regions could no longer be described as boggy wastelands, and certainly in good seasons were covered by fields of waving corn where once the tops of reeds had swayed in the breeze. As the drainage took effect settlers moved on to the land and farms and cottages sprang up on the new lands. Hard work could be re-paid and rewarded by good crops. To all intents and purposes the objectives of the original charter as granted by Charles I had come to pass, as written in 1861:

In those places which lately presented nothing to the eyes of the beholders but great waters and a few reeds thinly scattered here and there, under the divine mercy might be seen pleasant pastures of cattle and kine, and many houses belonging to the inhabitants.

Generally, the improvements became more permanent and the risks of regression and loss less serious or at least less frequent. Over the decades the 'improvements' gradually went on with rivers flowing through artificial banks and often into new channels. But it is worth considering too the period of time from the demise of Vermuyden and his adventurers in the late 1600s to the situation that seemed so pleasant to the eyes of the industrializing and agriculturally improving Victorians. Vermuyden is the name that almost everyone associates with these great drainage schemes, but there were other and equally eminent engineers who followed. There were also other factors and issues that finally swept almost the last vestiges of these once great wildernesses from the map. Perhaps the most significant of the engineers was John Smeaton, born on 8 June 1724 in Whitkirk, four miles east of Leeds. Probably most famous for the iconic Eddystone Lighthouse, Smeaton worked in many areas of civil and mechanical engineering and these included fenland drainage. One of his major works was the drainage of Potteric Carr in South Yorkshire.

Draining South Yorkshire's Biggest Carr

Such is Vermuyden's reputation in bringing about the transformation of these landscapes that even today the drainage of all these areas, including, for example, Potteric Carr, is often mistakenly attributed to him. Potteric was the largest of the South Yorkshire carrs, lying west of the greater Humberhead Levels and at the edge of the Great South Yorkshire Fen. It covered around 4,250 acres of low-lying ground south-east of Doncaster. By the mid-1700s, the area had two drains running through the north-western area and into a small lake, the Old Eaa. From here the water flowed down a stream into the River Torne. The Torne was embanked for much of its length and the stream entered it via a sluice. A small area north of St Catherine's Well Stream, which was also embanked, was drained by the Huxterwell Drain and entered the Torne at the same sluice. Much of this area was still subjected to severe flooding and so consideration was given to the potential of establishing effective drainage and protection from inundation for the whole area. To this end the Corporation of Doncaster and one of the major landowners, William Dixon of Loversall, commissioned a feasibility report from Smeaton. He had previously submitted plans to drain Lochar Moss near Dumfries, though his plans had not been taken up. Smeaton visited Potteric in July 1762 and took a series of levels across the area. In September of that year he reported on two possible schemes. The first proposal was to take the water from a new main drain in the carr via a short tunnel under the ridge that carries the Doncaster to Balby road. The water would then flow in an open cut to meet with the River Don a little upstream of Friars Bridge. The second possibility was to lead the main drain or Mother Drain to an outfall on the Torne around three quarters of a mile below Rossington Bridge, entering via a sluice. The latter was to have doors directed towards the river but also a draw door on the landward side to hold water back in the event of drought. This second scheme was the simpler of the two but might incur objections from landowners downstream on the Torne if they felt that increased flooding might occur.

The levels survey indicated that the lowest ground of the carr was about five feet above the level of the River Torne. The general guidance for land drainage was that the water in the ditches and dikes should be at a minimum of two feet below the land surface. There would then be a fall for the drain of about three feet over three and a quarter miles. However, there seems to have been some sort of error in the surveys. Whereas the levels in the carr and the Torne were accurate, there was a problem with those across to the River Don. In actual fact the land at Friars Bridge, rather than being below Potteric Carr, was actually at about the same level. In other words there would be no fall. By November 1763 Smeaton's fees of £26-5s were paid and in January 1764 he was asked to prepare estimates for the works to be undertaken. He spent a further six days on site in March of that year at a charge of £1-8s-6d (one guinea plus 7s-6d expenses) to undertake the necessary additional work to produce the costs for the first scheme. Evidently it was the drain to the River Don that was the preferred option. Works of this nature required Parliamentary approval and so a petition went to Parliament in January 1765. The Town Clerk for Doncaster, Richard Sheppard, drew up the bill, and Smeaton presented evidence. The act was obtained in April 1765.

However, it seems that there was some suspicion that all was not well, for in May 1765 James Brindley, engineer, was asked by Doncaster Corporation to 'take a Levell of Potterick Carr to find which will be the most effectual way and method to drain the same'. He was paid a fee of eight guineas plus one guinea for travelling expenses from Barnsley. It is likely that one of the Commissioners named in the act, perhaps Thomas Tofield who lived nearby, had realized the errors in the levels. However, it appears that Smeaton had already been on site and was working up a detailed proposal for the second scheme. It was this more detailed proposal that was eventually undertaken. The River Torne was to be diverted in a long cut through a new bridge to be built adjacent to the existing Rossington Bridge. The latter would accommodate the new Mother Drain. The outfall would be built on Doncaster Corporation land to avoid any legal issues with adjacent landowners. This was around half a mile upstream from the point originally chosen. There were problems with this in that the gradient of the fall, so important in major drainage projects, was reduced to around five inches per mile. To compensate for this, Smeaton decided that the Mother Drain would have a considerable bottom width of about eighteen feet and be carried on a horizontal plane with a depth of six feet; two feet below the river level at the outfall. The new channel for the River Torne was to be at least twenty feet wide and with bank slopes of not more than one-in-one. He also planned to take the water that ran into the carr from the 'uplands' (not a large catchment) via catch-water drains around the edge of the main body of the carr. The work to completion was then reasonably straightforward, undertaken in three stages. The first phase was completed by 1768, with the new Rossington Bridge built, the new Torne channel cut, and the upstream channel enlarged with raised and extended embankments. The Division Drain and the Lady Bank Drain were enlarged and the Mother Drain was cut to the old course of the River Torne.

Following the successful completion of the first stage there was a delay as land in the northern part of Potteric Carr was allotted and enclosed with an award of 1771. This was the land also owned by Doncaster Corporation, but presumably with common rights attached. The second phase of work commenced in 1772 and was completed in 1774. This included the extension of the Mother Drain under old Rossington Bridge, the building of the sluice, the cutting of Rossington Drain and the enlargement and extension northwards of Huxterwell Drain. In total there were around four-and-a-half miles of new cut on the River Torne, the same for the new Mother Drain, and about eight miles of other cuts.

John Smeaton

Smeaton's approach to Potteric Carr and its drainage accords with some of the main principles of fenland and carr drainage. The scheme separates what are termed the 'living waters' of the rivers and tributary streams from the 'land waters'; the latter being those generated by rainfall actually within the site to be drained. This is done by a process of embanking the watercourses and straightening or deepening the channels to improve their flow characteristics. The intention is to stop them overflowing on to the land in times of flood and to remove water from the area as quickly as possible. This reduces the necessary function and capacity of the drains within the target area. They have to deal with the rainfall on to the site itself and any smaller amounts of water flowing in from higher ground which cannot be taken directly to the main river. These drains must then have enough capacity to carry the water off the site and should discharge downstream as far as is possible. In order to prevent a backflow reversing up the drains when the river is in spate, a sluice may be necessary. However, there is often a need to ensure some water supply for agricultural needs, and so some capacity to hold back the flow may be necessary. But the prime agricultural demand is to lower the water-table and so the water levels in the drains are to be kept several feet below the level of the surrounding ground. The resultant storage capacity in the drainage system means that there is a buffering effect during high flows and peak discharges are smoothed out. It seems that for many of the engineers they made their detailed plan and designs based on personal experience. For some of the complicated issues of channel flow and water movement there were and are no simple or easy answers. Smeaton noted:

1. Flow occurs within the full cross-section of a channel even when the bottom of the channel lies below the level of the outlet; i.e. there is no 'dead water'.

2. As an equal quantity of water must, in the same channel, pass in a given time through every section, the velocity will vary inversely as the area of the section.

3. For a given flow the greater the velocity (under equal circumstances) the greater will be the gradient, and vice-versa.

4. For a given cross-sectional area and gradient, the flow increases with the ratio (R) of area to wetted perimeter; that is, the hydraulic mean depth.

5. This last fact justifies the extra expense of making drains with a horizontal bottom, rather than a sloping one, where gradients are small, and for digging the bottom below the level of water at the outfall, as at Potteric Carr.

The above were set down in a letter to Tofield and Grundy with regards to an enquiry about drainage at Deeping Fen in 1770. The

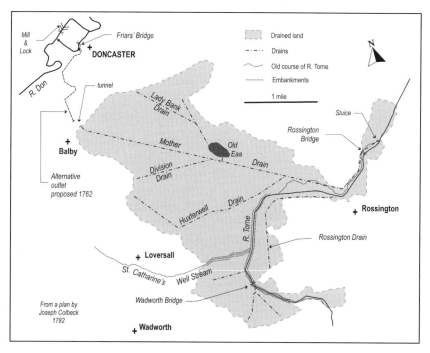

Potteric Carr Drainage after Skempton

approach, combined with the basic principles, will generally achieve the effective drainage of a fen or carr. This was also undertaken at a time before detailed calculations of relationships determining flow in channels had been developed.

Smeaton and the Fens of Yorkshire and North Lincolnshire

Whilst working on the successful drainage of the greatest of the South Yorkshire Carrs, Potteric Carr, Smeaton also turned his attention first to Holderness (in 1763), Hatfield Chase (in 1764), and then Adlingfleet Level near Trent Falls (in 1772). In Holderness he worked with engineer John Grundy on a scheme to improve the drainage of around 11,000 acres of low ground in the Hull Valley. Grundy was the engineer working on a new sluice at Deeping Fen in Lincolnshire. At Adlingfleet the construction of a comprehensive drainage scheme in 1772 removed flooding from around 5,000 acres of low ground, some of which was permanently under water. He had first visited the site in 1755 at the request of the landowner at Haldenby Manor. His suggestion at the time was that in order to avoid the expense of the necessary Parliamentary Act for the construction of new drains, the existing drains were to be enlarged and the Ousefleet sluice re-built. John Grundy had also visited the nearby estate at Eastoft in 1759 to report to the owner, Mr Marmaduke Constable. His view was that the land had sufficient fall to facilitate drainage but that the existing drains were too narrow and had too many bends. However, there were problems in implementing any improvement since numerous landowners were involved and the scheme would come under the Court of Sewers. Without an individual Act of Parliament the difficulties might be too complex to be overcome. His suggestion was to leave any attempt on this bigger improvement for now, and to build a wind-driven scoop, engine or windmill to lift water off the land directly.

The ultimate solution was a collaboration of the major

landowners in presenting a bill to Parliament for the necessary act in order to progress the works. Smeaton, working with a detailed survey and map from Charles Tate, reported on the scheme in December 1764. Whilst the existing network of drains might be satisfactory improved by enlarging and straightening the drains and rebuilding the sluice, it was advocated that a new drain be cut from the Green Bank in the south to an outfall on the River Trent. With a lower low tide here this meant a better fall and the sluice could remain open for longer than at Ousefleet. The lowest points in the land to be drained were at Haldenby Common (four miles from the outfall) and at Eastcroft Moor (five-and-a-half miles from the outfall). The calculation suggested a fall of about one foot per mile and a drain-water level at around two feet below the land, all in all very satisfactory for effective drainage. At this time Adlingfleet had no major river across its boundaries, the whole site being very flat and the old course of the River Don having been diverted by Vermuyden. The latter had made little attempt to effect any drainage of this area and so Smeaton's scheme required barrier banks to be raised along the southern and south-western boundaries to prevent flooding from outside the area. These effectively enclosed the area, with the natural levees of the old River Don raised to the east and the Whitgift drainage system to the west. This meant that the only incoming water was from rainfall on the area itself and drainage could be effected by simply taking this water off. The advice was heeded and the Act of Parliament for the major works to the River Trent was obtained in March 1767. Smeaton was paid £28-16s-4d for his fees and expenses. The work was undertaken by John Grundy and completed in 1769, and the Enclosure Commissioners made their award in 1772. This set out the details of the now drained land field by field, together with the Mother Drain and the embankments. The total cost of drainage this area of around 5,000 acres was about £7,000. The main drain, nearly six miles long, involved around 170,000 cubic yards of material excavated at around three pence per cubic yard. There were just over twelve miles of lesser drains generally about six feet deep and about five feet wide at the bottom.

Smeaton was also working on improvements to the drainage of Hatfield Chase, Vermuyden's first really major fenland scheme. It was over 100 years since the original undertaking, and the tax revenue from the 14,000 acres allotted to Vermuyden and his fellow adventurers (the 'scotted' land) and from the 3,000 acres allotted to local landowners (the 'decreed' land) was largely spent on the ongoing maintenance of the rivers, channels, drains and embankments. There was also the need to pay off the initial capital expenditure, but as was often the case these costs were rarely met. One issue that arose was the restriction of water flow at Misterton Soss. Vermuyden had built a tidal sluice at Misterton with embankments between the sluice and the outfall, and a further barrier bank between the north side of the River Idle and higher ground near to Misson. The River Trent had already been embanked to prevent high tides flooding over into the adjacent land. With the river in flood the rise in high tide could be fourteen to sixteen feet above normal at this point. These works ensured that tidal waters and freshwater floods were kept off the lower grounds north of the barrier bank. The Carrs of Gringley and Misteron had also been converted into 'summer grounds', i.e. pasture land flooded only in winter and so available to stock grazing at other times. To relieve the constriction of the flow Smeaton recommended additional sluice doors to be constructed and the cut widened to allow this. The water would rise to a lower height and the waters would also run off more quickly and the carr pasture lands would be improved. However, the benefits of the proposal were largely for lands outside the scheme, i.e. the carrs, and so the landowners proceeded only with the raising of the banks. Later, in the 1790s, the Everton, Gringley and Misterton Carrs were completely drained by the engineer William Jessop and the additional sluices as originally designed by Smeaton were included. They were eventually replaced by a new sluice and floodwater pumps in the 1900s.

The Snow Sewer was an old watercourse enlarged and extended as a main drain to take water from the carrs south of the Isle of Axholme. It runs for six miles and has an outfall to the River Trent at Owston. There were problems with the water overflowing at high tide and Smeaton re-constructed the banks and sluices to resolve this. Another problem was with the flooding that still occurred with the River Torne during periods of high rainfall. Vermuyden had constructed a new cut that ran north-east and with four right-angled bends close to Hirst Priory. At this point it picked up the water from the short main drain and carried this east via the 'South River' to an outfall with a sluice on the River Trent at Althorpe. The adventurers' scheme had also had a main drain called the New Idle, which flowed from Idle Stop, under the Torne at Tunnel Pit and so to Dirtness Bridge. From there as the 'North River' it went north-eastwards to Hirst Priory and to a large sluice at Althorpe. Following the Vermuyden project another link had been cut between the North and South Rivers at Hirst Priory. The idea of this was that if under severe flood the two channels would each flow at their maximum capacity and ensure the most effective discharge. Smeaton identified problems of the lack of height in some of the embankments and also the lack of sufficient depth in parts of the new cut River Torne. Various suggestions to improve the situation had already been made, but the costs were considered prohibitive and the works would have necessitated a specific Act of Parliament. However, by the 1770s there was a renewed enthusiasm to undertake the necessary works and surveys were carried out. In 1776, Smeaton reported in detail on the problems and issues of the River Torne drainage. In this report he points out that:

> as I understand that the whole Course of the proposed outfall Drain, lays thro' Parishes and Lordships wholly unconnected with the Participants concern in Hatfield Chase; in case Difficulties should arise in reconciling these different interests, it seem to me of consequence to that Body of Gentlemen, and the Country at present depending upon their Undertaking, to shew how these Levels of Hatfield Chase may be drained, in a very competent Manner, without going out of their own Boundary.

He goes on to explain how he proposed to achieve this. He was to cut a new and improved drain from Tunnel Pit to the Trent to carry off excess floodwater and to provide this with an effective outfall sluice. The project involved deepening the bed at key points, new cuts and the straightening and shortening of the channels at critical points. The embankments between the Torne Bridge and the Ross Bridge were also to be raised. The total costs were estimated at around £13,500 for the actual works, excluding legal fees and so on. The works were to a large degree, but not totally, successful. Further improvement had to be undertaken at a later date by Matthias Scott, the Surveyor of Works who had already been involved in the enlarging of the North River from Crowle Bridge to Althorpe in 1773. These additional works were probably omitted by Smeaton on grounds of cost. Having obtained the necessary Act of Parliament in 1783, Scott designed a new cut in the north to Keadby, and a new sluice and thirty-foot-wide cut. The work was carried out by Scott's successor Samuel Foster, largely following Smeaton's original plans for the new Torne and the South Idle drain. There were significant improvements though in the provision of separate outfalls at Althorpe to the River Trent. Along with widening the existing drains the new works had included ten miles of new cuts, considerable new embanking, three new sluices and a number of new bridges. The total cost incurred over the period from around 1776 to 1789 was about £23,000, and now in Smeaton's words Hatfield Chase had been drained 'in a very competent manner'. Although more works would be undertaken in the centuries that followed, the combined efforts of Smeaton, Brindley, Scott, Foster and Grundy sealed the final fates of many of the wetlands that survived Vermuyden and his adventurers.

Drainage Across the Wider Yorkshire Fens

The greatest challenge was in draining the huge floodlands and raised mires at the core of the great Yorkshire Fen, and its achievement ranks as one of the great engineering feats of the time. However, there was also a great deal of activity happening across the wider Fen and in the wetlands that were strewn along each of the constituent river valleys. In the Ancholme Valley in 1637 a new cut was dug between Bishopsbridge to the Humber, and at South Ferriby a new tidal sluice was constructed. These were intended to improve navigation and to control flooding, but were only partially successful. The carrs of Routh and Swine were successfully drained but the lands further north were still vulnerable to flooding. By the nineteenth century the Beverley–Barmston Drain and the Holderness Drain were cut and the River Hull was dredged from Driffield to Hull, and many of the problems were solved. Across Holderness there were still numerous post-glacial meres present in medieval times, and they were considered valuable for fowling and for fishing. However, many of these were drained during the 1200s and 1300s, with the objective of agricultural improvement. The major period of drainage of the meres was the 1500s and 1600s, after which only the largest, Hornsea Mere, remained by 1858.

In the Vale of York Wallingfen survived until the cutting of the Market Weighton Canal in the late 1700s and the River Derwent has retained intact washlands to this day. The Lincolnshire Marsh was less problematic to reclaim. With alleviation and coastal sediment accretion, extensive storm beaches and the building of the sea-bank, there was little need for more than local drainage channels to be cut.

From the 1700s onwards a further impetus to drainage and reclamation came from the drive to enclose and thus 'improve' open common land and 'wastes' through Parliamentary Enclosures. Each area targeted had an individual Act of Parliament and the process continued until well into the 1800s. This not only facilitated reclamation of the former wetlands but also created a whole new landscape and social structure. The open fields, with the nationally notable exception of around the Isle of Axholme, had largely gone, to be replaced by dispersed farms scattered around the older nucleated villages and other settlements. As part of the process of improvement around the tidal zones of the Humber Estuary there was applied what is believed to be a unique system of reclamation: 'warping'. This was basically the embankment of fields to retain mineral-rich sediments carried by tidal floodwaters. It was undertaken for a number of years and was used extensively in the region during the 1800s and early 1900s. The process effects two major changes. The first is that it buries the unproductive peat soils under a layer of rich mineral soil. The second change is that over time it raises the areas of land above the level of regular floods. This system was called 'flood-warping' and there was an alternative where flood management was difficult to apply, called 'cart-warping'. As the name suggests this was where the silt was carried on to the land by cart, and was similar to the use of mineral-rich sand transported to land improvement sites in the south-west of England such as along the Camel Estuary in Cornwall. Warping was applied to large areas along the lower Trent Valley, to the northern parts of Thorne Moors and to the lower reaches of the Vale of York. Thomas Bunker in 1876 described the process of warping:

> It appears that considerable tracts of poor land and moor are very low, in fact lower than high water mark at spring tide. Advantage is taken of this by raising a bank perhaps 10 feet high round a field of perhaps 20 to 40 acres and allowing the tidal waves to flow from the river by means of a large drain into the field; at high water, when the current ceases, a large portion of the mud held in suspension settles on the land, and the comparatively clear water runs off as the tide ebbs. This mode of proceeding is continued for some years and the result is the deposit of as good a soil as need be wished for.

As the major flood management and the big drainage schemes kicked in, farming in the wider landscape did its part too. Across the entire region the lowland fields cut out of open fields and waste by improvers had drainage ditches or 'wet hedges' dug around them. And then within the fields themselves there were increasingly effective drains and drainage systems imposed. By the 1800s, lime and marl were being applied to improve soil condition and fertility, and by the twentieth century the period of intensive agri-industrial farming added synthetic fertilizers and other chemicals to drive production upwards. One of the most important people involved in drainage of the area in the nineteenth century was the engineer Makin Durham of Thorne. Locally he was known as 'the second Vermuyden' and was also 'by far the largest proprietor on Thorne Moors'. Durham was born in 1805 and died seventy-seven years later in March 1882. He began work as an apprentice to Richard Pilkington, the Thorne surveyor, who was particularly involved in enclosures across northern England, and later took over Pilkington's practice. However, Durham retained a strong local interest and concentrated on practical and financial matters of drainage and land reclamation in the Thorne and Hatfield area. In effect he oversaw the effective and scientifically based drainage of lands across the region. Locally focused Acts were passed and local finance was raised to undertake the work. With the first Dun Drainage Act in the 1830s, Durham was made the Commissioner for an extensive area of riverside land between Bentley, Doncaster, Stainforth and Fishlake. These lands were to be drained and the Commissioners made their award in April 1839, with Durham appointed as the engineer to both make and then maintain the necessary works 'of great importance to the district'. Durham was also appointed as engineer to the Corporation of the Level of Hatfield Chase, a post that he had held for their predecessors the Trustees of Decreed Lands. He undertook the design and the engineering of the drainage of the Levels into North and South Districts, each drained by steam-driven pumping engines. His projects also included drainage schemes along the Went and in other areas too. Overall, his contribution was, effectively, to mop up much of the wetland that remained after the earlier great schemes and the piecemeal land improvement under the enclosures.

We leave this phase, which might be called 'The Great Draining', and move on to the twentieth century. With the main drainage accomplished this was not the end of the process, since some intractable sites still hung on, many clinging tenaciously to life until the 1940s, when American technology with tracked vehicles and tractors bled the last vestiges of life out of the Yorkshire Fens. There then followed the excesses of government-funded intensive agriculture in the post-war years, which nailed the lid down on the coffin of the old fenland scene. Only in a very few places could nature remain but isolated and emasculated, until finally, at the end of the twentieth century, the pendulum of change began to swing back towards a more sustainable future.

Chapter Seven

How Yorkshire's Fens Fared from the Victorians to Today

The Final Stages of Reclamation

From the late 1800s and through the 1900s we witness the final death throes of the fens in both the northern and southern regions. Increasingly isolated in the landscape, desiccated and also exploited for peat, the remaining sites clung on, a few hundred acres here and there, usually by dint of their intractable physical nature or simply by chance. The biggest remaining across the county were the once vast Thorne and Hatfield Moors in South Yorkshire. Gradually, however, lowered water-tables and intensive farming led to the destruction of soils in the surrounding areas. These were often simply blown away as dust and the inevitable shrinkage and lowering of the ground surface followed. Traditional uses of the remaining sites ceased and combined with low water led to ecological successions with fen turning to wet woodland and meadow to scrub. A few remaining sites gradually became of interest to local naturalists but they were still being exploited for peat fuel and then peat moss litter. Some areas were abandoned during the First World War and the Depression years, but with the outbreak of war again in 1939 and the advent of newly imported technologies for farming almost everything was swept away in the post-war rush to 'improve'. In the Vale of York areas such as Wheldrake Ings, Askham Bog and Skipwith Common still hung on, and further south in the Humberhead Levels Thorne and

Hornsea Mere

Hatfield Moors clung on, though radically transformed. Elsewhere such as in Holderness and the Vale of Pickering all major fens had long since been erased, leaving just Hornsea Mere as a marker of a vanished landscape in the former, and a few small wetter sites in the latter. The great carrs of the Doncaster area had all slipped from the map but Potteric was to re-emerge in a remarkable story of recovery.

A Unique Resource

There is a further depth of knowledge that gives a fascinating insight into the ecology of these landscapes in times past. Unfortunately, as the contemporary wildlife of the regions has been decimated, so too has the unique evidence held within the peat archive been largely destroyed. Basically, within a saturated peat bog there are lots of organic acidic chemicals that result from the slow breakdown of vegetation, and there is very little oxygen. This means that organic material trapped within the peat layers is preserved, sometimes for thousands of years. The materials may be specimens or usually fragments of insects, or the pollen and tissues of plants. Human remains, often from ceremonial killings, also turn up from time to time, and are

HATFIELD CHACE DRAINAGE.

Madam,
Sir,

Doncaster, May 20th 1818

I am to inform you, that your Proportion of the *Second* Assessment, laid towards defraying the Expences of the said Drainage, amounts to the Sum of £ 20 . 12 . 10 which you will be pleased to pay into the Bank of Messrs. Yarborough, Childers, Foljambe, and Parker, in Doncaster, on or before *Saturday* the *Thirteenth* Day of *June* next.

I am, Sir, Madam,

Your obedient Servant,

£. s. d.
20 . 12 . 10 ⎰
14 . 6 . 5
——————
42 .. 19 .. 3

W. Bright

Clerk.

Miss Ann Smelter.

Hatfield Chase Drainage Assessment Notice Served to Ann Smelter of Richmond Hill, 1818 equally well preserved. However, careful and meticulous piecing together of the evidence from these remains of animals and plants can provide a unique insight into the landscape, ecology and climate prevailing across these areas in times past. This palaeo-ecological and palynological research is one of our most powerful tools in unravelling a lost ecology, and researchers such as Paul Buckland and Nikki Whitehouse have unearthed remarkable evidence at Thorne Moors of how and why the landscape has changed over the millennia. There is too little space to go into this work in detail, but much of it is published, and it is of global significance. In the Northern Fen it is the core peat bog sites of Thorne and Hatfield that have attracted most attention, whilst the wider landscape has been considered relatively much less. The reason is simple: that the wider landscape was swept away so much earlier and it was only the huge peat masses that were so intransigent that they have remained long enough to be available to contemporary researchers. It is worth finishing this section with a description of the sheer size and wetness of the great peat domes of Thorne Moors from Woodruffe-Peacock in 1920–1921. The description is of the variation in volume and hence height with seasonal conditions, attributed to the very wet core of the bog.

> In rainy seasons . . . its central mass was feet higher when full and swollen with water than in dry summers with normal rainfall, as it lifted as it swelled on the principle of in summer the dry and in winter the wet sponge. This I have over and over again observed personally from the great central Railway line, as in wet times nothing on its northern side was visible which could be clearly distinguished in dry summer weather. In 1875 it was estimated that the winter rise and summer fall of the bog was about six feet, in an abnormally wet season in the sixties, eight feet.

The Fate of the Northern Fens

Remote from centres such as Cambridge and its university, the Northern Fens seem to lack the rich literature and awareness of their southern counterparts. Apart from occasional forays by the Yorkshire Naturalists' Union or the various Doncaster naturalists and a few passionate protectors such as William Bunting, there was little written or celebrated about this lost fenland. Even the accounts we have tend to focus on the still present though severely battered sites like Thorne and Hatfield Moors. In recent decades there has emerged a new awareness of the importance of these core sites, and there has been an intensity of research to parallel that at Wicken Fen in the south. There is far too much even to summarize here, but perhaps just a taste will whet the appetite. There is a vast literature on the archaeology of the Humber region and especially its wetlands co-ordinated by Robert Van de Noort and his team, formerly at the University of Hull and now at Exeter, and palaeo-ecological studies at Thorne and Hatfield have been driven by Paul Buckland and others such as Nicki Whitehouse, both formerly at Sheffield University, the latter now at Queen's Belfast. These long-term and often intensive studies have placed the core sites and the landscape history of the region firmly on the map. However, there have been other major contributions too, notably from people at Doncaster Museum – Colin Howes, Peter Skidmore and Martin Limbert, who with a team of co-workers from the local natural history society have researched and recorded diligently the history and natural history of the sites. There have also been individual researchers and writers such as Martin Taylor who have considered the River Don and also Thorne Mere and their place in the landscape and its history, and of course the great regional and local antiquaries such as Abraham de la Pryme and Joseph Hunter. In recent years there has also been new work and exciting projects developing around Sutton Common, a northern equivalent of Flag Fen in Cambridgeshire. At this site and at others, the Carstairs Trust and Ian Carstairs have taken a lead. Yet despite all this, the Northern Fens have always had a problem of a wider identity and really of an identifiable unity, and in this they differ significantly from those of East Anglia. Furthermore, they differ too in their relationship with their catchment and their uplands. The Humber Levels and the great Northern Fens are separated from their wider central catchment by the Magnesian Limestone ridge that runs north to south across England, and here is cut through by the river at the Don Gorge. Beyond Conisbrough, however, the landscape opens up again and the great wetlands extended north-west along the Dearne Valley into Old Moor and Ferrymoor, both extensive medieval wet moors. These are now enjoying a re-birth at the hands of mining subsidence, post-mining recovery of water-tables and the custodianship of the RSPB. Further to the south-west the River Don cuts through Rotherham and towards Sheffield, through what was Lake Meadowhall at the Tinsley Viaduct, along what in medieval times was still impassable wetlands in the flat valley bottom of the Lower Don Valley, and then along Sheffield's five rivers to join a vast upland wetland of peat bog, fen and mire across the Peak District and the South Pennines. At Rotherham, the River Don splits, with the valley of the Rother tracking southwards to beyond Chesterfield, and again this was a great wetland valley with the largest fen and marsh in Derbyshire situated at Killamarsh (Killa's Marsh). This intimate connectivity has never been fully appreciated and the region, unlike the Southern Fens, has lacked a unifying identity. Through history though, from the very earliest times, it did act as a significant barrier and boundary in terms of its physical presence and the difficulty in crossing it, and in the transfer of culture. At the same time, the rivers themselves acted as arteries for movement and trade.

The complexity of the Humber wetlands and hence of the Northern Fens is manifest further to the east too. In Yorkshire, the great wetlands extended up the Hull Valley to Holderness and along the River Aire towards Leeds, and the River Ouse and the Derwent to York. In Lincolnshire, the River Trent cuts through and leads to Nottinghamshire and Sherwood Forest. The River Ancholme runs in the broad valley between the Lincolnshire Edge in the west and the Lincolnshire Wolds in the east. Along the coastline around the Humber Estuary the Northern Fens had connectivity with the Southern Fens through the extensive coastal marshes of Lincolnshire. The region retains a degree of this, though much reduced, along the coastal flats, dunes and salt marshes.

Lacking any overall recognition or account of the region, to understand what happened over the last century or so we must turn to the various individual accounts. For example, in 1991 Catherine Caufield wrote a short book called *Thorne Moors*, based on interviews with key individuals, especially the famously rude and irascible William Bunting, Thorne's equivalent of Wicken's politically incorrect James Wentworth-Day. Born in Barnsley in 1916, the son of a greengrocer, Bunting left school at sixteen to become an engineer's fitter. His job was to make and mend machines and tools. He later moved into more exciting and less conventional jobs as a courier for the *Reynolds News*, a left-wing Sunday paper, and was involved in smuggling money and messages to the anarchists during the Spanish Civil War. This was

Marshmen clearing weed

followed in the Second World War by various undercover operations for the British government in places such as Yugoslavia. At the end of the war, William Bunting and his family settled in Thorne and he became fascinated by the Moors, their history and their wildlife. He died after a long illness in 1995.

Bunting presented the image of what he himself described as 'a bad-tempered old sod'. I suspect that like Wentworth-Day in the Southern Fens, Bunting was bitter and disappointed by the impact of the modern social and political creed on this irreplaceable environment, and the unwillingness in the early days, or inability later on, of either academics or the conservation movement to do much about it. Furthermore, he believed most sincerely, and often had evidence to prove at least some of it, that much of the damage and the exploitation for private and individual gain were in fact illegal. In the case of his beloved Thorne Moors, Bunting was convinced that transfers from common rights and ownership to private interests, especially in the 1800s, were illegal. Not only was this the case, but because of vested interests in both mineral rights and in the mid-1900s the peat industry, the trail was deliberately and illegally covered up. This, he felt, was why all his efforts were blocked at every end and turn. Of course, to his reasoning, the local authorities and their officers and the public utilities and the agencies were all in cahoots; it was all conspiracy and bribery. The problem with Bunting's attitude was that whilst he had a very strong point and a significant amount, though by no means all, of what he claimed was true, he often did not discriminate in his ire towards foe and potential friend. He was often deliberately rude and even threatened violence simply to test people's resolve, and of course as a result many ran a mile. But in many ways, whilst huge and irreparable damage was done despite Bunting's efforts, much of what has survived is because of his passionate campaigning. He frequently took major utilities to court over what he felt were illegal acts, and to annoy them even more he often won and did so publicly. It was not only for Thorne that Bunting campaigned, but for the remnants of Potteric Carr too, appearing at the Public Inquiry for the proposed M18 motorway.

At the end of a typically long presentation by Bunting in the quasi-judicial arena of the inquiry, the long-suffering inspector apparently asked Bunting if there was anything he could tell the Minister in order to help him decide on this particularly difficult case. I've been told that Bunting's response was along the lines of 'Yes, you can tell him to **** off back down south.' Diplomacy was not Bunting's forte, but then perhaps he had a point.

In order to understand the transformations in this landscape, once the third-largest fenland in England, we need to consider the issues of perceptions of wetlands and values. This is especially so in the Humber Levels, where in the shadow of the coal industry rather than the refined spires and colleges of Cambridge there was always the latent view that 'Where there's muck there's brass.' In the absence of a good economic use of a site or of land, there was clearly something seriously amiss. Given this prevailing view from the 1800s until the late 1900s, it is perhaps surprising that anything at all survived. Wicken held on in the south because of the early interest and its accessibility to entomological collectors; Thorne and Hatfield survived, though seriously damaged, because they were simply so big and intractable. Without Bunting and then other campaigners, they would surely have gone completely by the end of the twentieth century.

Thorne and Hatfield Moors

These two core sites are the main remains of the vast Humber Levels at the heart of what I call the great Northern Fens. Thorne, Goole and Crowle Moors, together with Hatfield Moors, are the remnant of the primeval wetland across the Humber or Humberhead Levels, with a history extending back over several thousand years. Together they cover around 3,318 hectares or 8,201 acres, forming the largest complex of lowland raised bog in Britain (but reduced from the original area of around 2,000 square kilometres). Today a large area of former peat workings is being managed by Natural England as a National Nature Reserve, and this includes parts of Crowle Moor that are owned and managed by the Lincolnshire Trust for Nature Conservation. When wetness allows the abandoned peat workings to revert to bog, these areas provide habitat for a rich diversity of fauna and flora with huge numbers of rare and unusual species. The whole area is badged by Natural England as the Humberhead Peatlands and the two main component areas are Thorne Moors, located north of the M180 motorway and east of the M18, and Hatfield Moors, lying south of the M180. Thorne Moors are still extensively wet, whereas Hatfield in recent times has been mostly very dry. In the 1990s, the then

Marsh Helleborine

Chief Executive of Natural England, Derek Langslow, was able to state:

> Thorne and Hatfield Moors, on the South Yorkshire–Humberside border, are the last remnants of a vast area of peat bog and fen that once covered much of the land around this part of the Humber estuary. It is the largest area of peat bog in lowland England.
>
> We stand at a historic moment. Peat has been taken from the moors for centuries – with little thought for the future. Now, following an agreement reached between English Nature and Levington Horticulture plc, we can start to rebuild.

The Moors have over 600 species of plants recorded and more than 3,000 species of invertebrates. These include numerous rarities and some almost unique to this area. Species include a population of nightjars that is of European significance, large numbers of adders, breeding nightingales and rare butterflies such as the Large Heath. Plants include bog rosemary, cranberry, round-leaved sundew and many more.

A Little History

Thorne Moors has been described as an unfortunate but 'classic' example of nature conservation and archaeological legislation failing to protect the archaeological and palaeo-environmental resource of the area. Having been severely affected by the drainage schemes of Vermuyden and those who followed, the once huge, double-domed raised bog was gradually encroached upon along the 'cables' of the implanted immigrant Dutch settlers: typically narrow, linear fields with ditches or hedges to either side run in parallel groups into the outer moor. The same pattern can be seen in the landscapes of reclaimed peat bogs in lowland areas of northern Europe and especially in Germany and Holland. People had extracted peat for domestic use as fuel since the earliest times, certainly from the medieval period, but most likely since the Romans or before. However, the scale of the cutting was small in relation to the resources and it was also a time of active peat growth. By the early 1800s William Harrison, a local botanist, a miller by trade, described to a friend how when he had moved to Thorne 'he could stand on his threshold and see Crowle Church across the Moors, but such had been the rapid rise of the surface in a comparatively short period, that the sacred edifice had become obscured from view'. By the 1880s the peat was being cut commercially for animal bedding and the Thorne Moors Improvement Company leased the Moors to a number of peat-extraction businesses. The first task as always was to drain the areas to be cut – not an easy task as the bog was still incredibly wet. The ditch diggers needed to wear 'fen boards' on their feet to stop them sinking in to the mire. Eventually the cut peat was taken off along paths constructed by tipping clinker from nearby blast-furnaces to stabilize the site. Shortly afterwards a Dutch company began cutting canals into the Moor and taking peat off by barges towed by horses, and then later a railway was built across the site to facilitate even easier removal.

Peat cutting necessitates drainage, and the lowered water-table changes the ecological conditions. With many of the animals and plants adapted to live in a peat bog being those specialized to an extreme and harsh environment, any major alteration may lead to loss and extinction. The rare mire pill beetle, for example, lives under the surface of wet peat and feeds on the leaves of moss. Change its habitat and it cannot adapt. The Rannoch rush is one of Britain's most rare plants and was discovered on Thorne Moors in 1831, but within fifty years it was lost due to the drainage. In the wet peat you can find its remains in abundance, but to see the living plant in Britain you would now need to travel to Rannoch Moor in Perthshire. Thus the process of extinction and the inexorable change in the peat bog due to drying out happens and is to a considerable degree irreversible. Even if the site were rewetted, how would a plant like the Rannoch rush get back – by train, perhaps? However, the peat cutting during the late nineteenth and early twentieth centuries had a big impact, but this was at least limited by the inability to dig too deep. Part of the diggers' legacy was to leave behind a series of abandoned cuts and wet trenches that quickly re-colonized and re-vegetated to create a mosaic of rich wildlife habitats. The clinker tracks even helped the establishment of a base-loving alkaline fen and areas of base-rich grassland. Peat was cut by hand in the traditional ways and hauled from the Moors in horse-drawn barges or carts. Intensification, mechanization and railway transport were to change all this, and by the time Bunting arrived in Thorne the future of the Moors was truly in the balance. At this time the conventional wisdom of the conservation agencies and of leading academics on peat bog ecology was that Thorne was indeed already wasted. The view was that this rather unappealing northern wasteland had been so badly affected by peat cutting and by farming that it was now of little value and not worth saving. Also at the time the conservation legislation was so weak as to be anaemic, and bodies such as the Nature Conservancy Council, whilst well meaning, were toothless tigers and as now always grossly under resourced. Often unable to act even if it did recognize a problem, Bunting of course viewed this as at best weakness and feebleness and at worst the result of conspiracy and bribery.

So despite Bunting's claims about the interest and value of the Moors, when the local authorities across what was to become South Yorkshire decided in the 1960s to tip ashes from coal-fired power stations and perhaps municipal waste too, it was considered an inherently good thing to do. At one sweep it would resolve a problem of waste disposal and also turn a waste land into a potential asset in the form of a regional airport. Originally put forward in 1962, and then again in 1969, the idea received considerable support. The airport proposal was again revived in 1971, and with the new South Yorkshire County Council established in 1974 the ash-tipping proposal was raised yet again, alongside a third proposal for an airport in 1976. By 1978 the reopening and upgrading of Thorne Colliery carried with it the threat of the disposal of coal mining waste over the area. Despite all the big guns of the establishment being set against him Bunting battled on against each of the proposals in turn, and eventually every one of them was defeated. Gradually Bunting's arguments were being heard and supported more widely and a nucleus of expert entomologists, botanists and palaeo-ecologists with an interest in the area was growing. Despite this the then Yorkshire Naturalists' Trust based in York, the main voluntary wildlife conservation body for the county, had in 1969 voted against objecting to the proposals to tip on the Moors. However, lobbied vigorously by Bunting and dragged out to the site to see it for themselves, the Trust changed tack and came out in support of the objectors. The Nature Conservancy Council was still to be won over and did not designate the site as a Site of Special Scientific Interest until 1970. Despite recognition that perhaps influenced future decisions on minerals but at the time had zero impact on the now industrial peat extraction by Fisons plc, the deterioration continued. In 1963 Fisons has taken over the British Moss Litter Company, the latter being the eventual successor to the Victorian Thorne Moors Improvement Company.

Bunting's Beavers: The First Environmental Activists

By 1971 the final phases of conflict over this most strongly contested landscape were drawing to a head. Fisons was now excavating several deep drains cutting right through the heart of the site and which were in effect poised to destroy the old Dutch Canal area, one of the richest remaining parts of the Moor. Expert opinion was that the unique fauna and flora could not withstand such a direct assault and the consequent lowering of summer water-tables. The result was one of the most amazing acts in conservation history, a little like the tearing down of enclosures around London commons in the mid-1800s or the fenland levellers before them. With a group of local naturalists, local residents and students from various northern universities (Sheffield, Manchester, York and

Nottingham), Bunting led the conservationists to direct action. This was the pioneer of Earth First and of Swampy and the rest. 'Bunting's Beavers', as they became known, trekked on to Thorne Moors almost every weekend during the spring and summer of 1972 and dammed the drains that Fisons had cut. With clay, stone, peat, logs and railway sleepers they held the flow of drainage water at bay to keep the precious water-tables as high as possible. The workers at Fisons tried to break the dams down and keep the drains flowing, but they were losing the battle. It was estimated that by the autumn some dozens of dams had been constructed, with individual ones up to forty feet thick. The activities made it to BBC television, after which Fisons dynamited eighteen of the dams, but undeterred the Beavers re-built them. Then, following major bad publicity, Fisons caved in and let the dams remain. They entered negotiations (from which Bunting, their *bête noire*, was of course excluded) with the Nature Conservancy Council and academics from the northern universities. In 1974 they agreed to protect a part of the site around the Dutch Canal and to repair and strengthen some of the dams built by Bunting's Beavers. The SSSI status placed upon the remaining 1,845 hectares of Thorne Moors in 1981 provided little more than notional protection to the site and especially to the archaeological and palaeo-environmental resource. Peat extraction continued more or less unhindered and neither archaeological remains within the peat or below the peat were given any protection. Existing planning permissions and decisions were unaffected by the SSSI designation. Here, as is the case for many other wetland sites in England, the licenses and planning permissions for peat extraction date mostly to the 1950s and the post-war revival in the peat industry. Then, in 1985, they sold 180 acres of the site to the Nature Conservancy Council for around £250,000 and it was declared a National Nature Reserve. Still too small and isolated an area to be viable and sustainable in the long term, the site remained under threat. Fisons and then Levington continued to drain the wider peatland and to opencast the peat. The consequences for the ecology and archaeology here were terrible, but the outcry continued and following a landmark conference held in the late 1980s at Doncaster Museum into the conservation of and the threats to peat sites the National Peat Campaign was established. This battled to change public opinion and to better inform the millions of gardeners whose hobby was destroying some of the most unique wildlife and archeological heritage that we possessed. Over the next two decades the peat extraction interests were ultimately bought out with some millions of pounds of public money. But even this followed what seemed to be very questionable deals behind the scenes between the conservation agency and the peat industry. Locals felt that a deal was being done to save the Somerset levels and to sacrifice Thorne and Hatfield, and a meeting was held in Thorne at a local school hall. Packed with hundreds of objectors and protestors from Thorne and from groups across the UK, the senior staff of the NCC ended up providing assurances that the site in its entirety would be purchased, though the peat miners still exacted concessions on being able to work out areas they considered already badly damaged beyond repair. There had for many years been contentious and controversial debates about how much peat they should be allowed to extract and whether areas that had been surface stripped might as well be worked down to the base. Some conservationists had done surveys for Fisons and advocated that at least one metre of peat should be left if there was to be any hope of regenerating a bog afterwards. On the other hand the archaeologists and palaeo-ecologists largely dismissed the idea of being able to re-create a bog, which they contend is valuable for its unique profile and the fossilized or preserved remains of plants and animals it contains. For agencies and legislation this idea of conservation has always been problematic, coming as it does somewhere in a no-man's land between protection of living organisms, solid geological features and heritage archaeology. For decades nobody seemed prepared to do anything meaningful to actually apply the law to protect this aspect of the natural landscape.

The key agreement was announced in 1992, but not actually signed until 1994. This meant the transfer of ownership or freehold of Thorne Moors from the peat producers (originally Fisons Plc and then Levington Horticulture, then later Scotts Company [UK] Ltd) to English Nature (the offspring of the NCC), now Natural England. This transfer was on the basis of a leaseback agreement so the peat producers continued peat extraction but leaving an average of a half-metre depth of basal peat to allow future restoration and conservation. Following the 1992 announcement around a thousand hectares of peatland was transferred to and has since been managed by the relevant agency. Central to this agreement is the concept that the raised mire of Thorne Moors can be restored after peat extraction has been completed. The main focus of the management was the idea, based on published recommendations on mire restoration, that worked areas could be regenerated if water loss could be minimized. This concept is as yet unproven but the prevention of water loss from the area has become a priority. Much to the annoyance of archaeologists and palaeo-ecologists, the management plans do not acknowledge the protection of the archaeological and palaeo-environmental resource. The rocky and often controversial road of the destruction and conservation of the Thorne Moors complex continued, though. In the mid-1990s what was then English Nature announced its plans to de-notify from Site of Special Scientific Interest (SSSI) status the wider buffer zone around the core peatlands of the National Nature Reserve. This was because they felt this buffer of cut and worked peat no longer contributed to the hydrological integrity of the site, a point hotly contested by the Yorkshire Wildlife Trust and the Thorne and Hatfield Moors Forum. Furthermore, much to the chagrin of the archaeologists, this overlooked the palaeo-archaeological interest that might remain. So the disputes over the site have gone on almost to the bitter end. Now, embedded in a wider Humberhead Peatlands designation, the process of gradual re-building goes slowly on. Much has been lost that can never be re-constructed, but there is hope that a core site will develop as a wonderful wildlife and even tourism resource. Who knows, maybe over a few hundred years a raised peat bog will once again rise above the surrounding landscape. It's a shame, but you and I won't be here to see it.

There is a vast literature on the issues described above and on the extensive surveys of ecology, palaeo-ecology and archaeology of the sites. Space here does not allow more detail, but perhaps the reader will be tempted to follow up and delve more deeply. You will not be disappointed. A good starting point are the *Thorne and Hatfield Moors Papers*, an occasional series edited by Martin Limbert at Doncaster Museum, or the huge volumes on the wetlands of the region written and edited by Robert Van de Noort (see the bibliography for further details).

A Re-birth

The loss of the Yorkshire and North Lincolnshire Fens, what I call the Great Northern Fen, together with the more widely known drainage of the Southern Fens of East Anglia, must be the greatest single ecological catastrophe that has ever occurred in England. It is therefore worth asking what the future might hold for this enigmatic landscape. First of all it must be recognized that we cannot recover what has been lost. Even today there are new species being discovered in the tiny and often tattered fragments of landscape that remain. Each of these is exciting, but they also act as a reminder that we have undoubtedly lost animals and plants that we did not even know we had. It has also become clear that as we can never reinstate the old fen, as much of what we have today is not sustainable in the long term. In a global environment of increasing food insecurity there will be a need to produce food, and much of this will of necessity be grown intensively. This is the world in which we live. However, there is a need for compromise for both ethical environmental reasons but also for harsh pragmatic reasons. If we wish to grow food sustainably and intensively in the Northern Fens, then we need summer water for irrigation and we need to avoid the worst of the possible damage and disruption from both winter and summer floods. Clearly the best way to achieve this involves working with the grain of nature and not against it. So in the future there will be wetlands that once again work for a living and work with local people. The new wetlands can also be a catalyst for local economic renewal, as they generate new crops and products and trigger tourism income and other related benefits. The old fen was an intimate mixing of nature and people to create a wonderful and rich environment. Perhaps the new fenlands can be the same.

There are now ambitious plans to reinstate sites in the Northern Fens centred on the Humberhead Peatlands and Potteric Carr. These are exciting projects, though even at their best they will nowhere near replace what we have lost. Of course, for the environment and the landscape not all can be recreated and much is lost forever. There is also always the shadow of the vagaries and fluctuations in public opinion, the resolution or otherwise of agencies and politicians, and increasingly the pressures of world markets for grains and for fuel crops. There can be no room, even now, for complacency. There is also talk of promoting these areas to lock up atmospheric carbon and so to combat climate change, to help climate-proof the region by storing floodwaters, and to drive

Spoonbill

the regional economy through associated leisure and tourism. However, in spite of a lot of talk and considerable money being spent on research programmes, there remain no effectively co-ordinated efforts to bring this about. There is still no wider vision to restore the landscape on the scale necessary, or indeed to embed this within a maximization of long-term economic gain. But surely this must come soon. As the RSPB have demonstrated at the nearby RSPB Dearne Valley, these new wetlands can be at the heart of both the economy and the community. One of the most exciting projects is at Wheldrake Ings to the south-east of York in the valley of the River Derwent. This is a major site and retains elements of the medieval farming systems which functioned in the wetter landscape. With careful management by a number of conservation bodies the location has grown into one of the richest wildlife sites in England. But I still feel that far more could be done to link these major projects together and to promote more effective community and business involvement and to grow regional nature-based tourism on the back of this. There is still a long way to go to make these projects genuinely sustainable.

Chapter Eight

Flesh from the Bones:

Yorkshire's Fenland and Peat Cutters

From the mid-1800s emerged peat extraction and processing industries, in some cases the final nail in the coffin of the peatlands and often the death throes of the fenlands. But even with this extraction, the history and culture mixed with older, local traditions. Ultimately industry and agriculture removed most peatlands, many lost to drainage and farming 'improvement' from the 1700s to the 1900s. Peat fell out of domestic use with firewood and then coal, gas, oil or electricity each becomming available and more convenient. Some small areas of industrial peat extraction for horticulture have lingered on, but mostly it has stopped. We now destroy other people's fens and peat bogs to import their peat to Britain. The final stages of this process in South Yorkshire became, as we have seen, a bitter *cause célèbre* for conservation in this disputed landscape.

Peat was worked on a small domestic scale for millennia, and the impacts were quite limited. There were few people and huge fenland landscapes to exploit. What's more, the peat was still building more rapidly than people could cut it. However, as the population grew and society moved towards industrialization and urbanization, the demands changed. New technologies swung into action to drain and improve these vast wetlands and 'waste-lands'. Peat cutting played its role in transformation of these landscapes. When the peat-based fens were drained, there was sometimes a deep peat resource that could be harvested and sold.

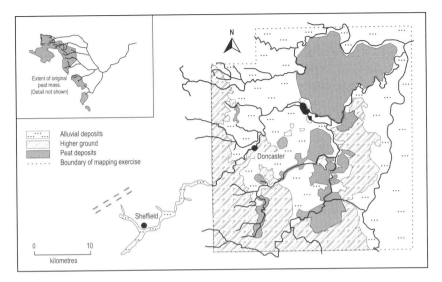

Humber peatlands

This was a bonus to the land improver. Furthermore, any peat that remained could be cut and burnt on the surface of the land as a fertilizer and soil improver to help cultivations and cropping. This was known as 'paring and burning', and with marling, claying, liming, warping and, of course, draining itself, was part of the armoury of the improver. Many of the peat areas were allocated to individuals on the enclosure of improved and drained areas of fen, and these were then worked as peat turbaries. In the Northern Fen the great peat mass of Thorne and Hatfield Moors and some of those in the Vale of York still remained reasonably intact in parts until well into the twentieth century.

Fenland Peat Cutting in Yorkshire and north Lincolnshire

As in the Southern Fens, the cutting and burning of peat fuel must have gone on in the Northern Fen for millennia. Certainly the Romans were cutting peat in sites like Askham Bog and Skipwith

Common. John Goodchild, writing in the early 1970s, or at least editing an otherwise anonymous contribution to the *South Yorkshire Journal*, described the history of peat cutting in and around the Thorne and Hatfield Moors area. Much of this was based on the remarkable find of an archive of documents and other materials at the ruined peat works on Thorne Moors. Without this find our knowledge would be very limited, and as the original journal is little known, much of the account is worth repeating here. There is much more written elsewhere but space here does not allow a more detailed account. Goodchild notes the absence of detailed accounts of the earlier periods but states that in the absence of any other easily available fuel in the area peat turf must have been important from an early date. He set about remedying some of the vacuum of information, based on the discovered archive. He suggests too that the peat when cut was transported out by boat and notes the difficulty in using any other form of transport in the area.

Peat fuel was clearly important across the area and there is evidence for Roman usage to the north around York, though areas perhaps used in the South Yorkshire and north Lincolnshire part of the Northern Fen must have long since been lost to agricultural improvement. Absence of evidence should not be taken as evidence of absence, and it would make sense for the Romano-British to have exploited this abundant fuel supply. Goodchild suggests that Thorne and Hatfield certainly became 'turf' moors in post-Roman times but notes that relatively little is known about this until the eighteenth century. However, he does give some interesting records of use of peat turf in York. In 1388 peat, or 'turbarum', was being brought into York by water to supplement the city's own turbary on the Tillmire near Heslington. He suggests that peat was not available from other sites on the main rivers near York and so additional supplies were needed, and the Yorkshire Fen was the obvious choice. It is thought that coal from the Leeds area was being burnt in Roman York, but there is little evidence of such early peat use. However, by the seventeenth century the amount of peat turf being consumed increased with improved transportation along the new Dutch River created for drainage, providing a deep navigable watercourse from Goole as far as Thorne. Transport by smaller boats was possible as far upstream as Doncaster as long as the tide was favourable. Such use is confirmed by references to a Thorne 'Keel man' (1687) and a Doncaster 'Waterman' (1717). Transport was still possible up the old Dun to Turnbridge until the late 1600s, when it had become too 'warped up', i.e. silted. By this time peat extraction from the moors was beginning to increase, drainage allowing access and turbary, and then agriculture following. In York in 1643 there was reference to the selling of turf when nine men were accused of 'selling turfs contrary to my Lord Mayor's price'. Admitting guilt, they were fined three-quarter pence each 'according to an Order made in the like case the 9th day of November 1593'. This latter reference was to four men reprimanded and fined for a similar offence. In the 1643 entry for fines paid to the Corporation of York it is stated that money was received 'of watermen for selling turves before the price was sett by my Lord Mayor 8/-'. The notes refer to the month of November so perhaps a time when the cold was making turf especially important. It is suggested that references indicate that

Peat wagon

peat was worked across a wide area of the old West Riding during the seventeenth century. There are references to 'Turf Mosses', to 'wayne leades of dryed peates', to the use of carts for carrying dried peat and to 'the turfpitt' from places such as Giggleswick, Thruscross, Barwick-in-Elmet, Bentham and Fishlake. In the latter case the notes refer to the theft in 1652 of 'one Catch loade of Turves & wood' with a total value of £7. This was by four men, one of whom was referred to as an 'Airmyn Waterman', and the 'Catch' was a ketch, one of the traditional open sailing trading barges that plied up and down these watercourses.

There is little detail on the actual organization of the turf cutting industry until the eighteenth century. As drainage allowed further encroachment into the great peat mass of the raised mire of Thorne, turf moors were worked from a series of cuts next to the canals that extended short distances into the bog. These mostly ran westwards and out of the Moor. There is reference on a plan of 1752 to 'The Cutt by Thorn into Trent used by the Tenants instead of the Old River Dun.' By 1790 this canal and drain was used by around thirty to forty boats carrying turf that was then transferred into Dun barges or ketches. Still called 'The Boating Dyke' in the 1970s, in 1817 it was known as 'the Ancient Drain and Canal called Boating Dyke'. Prior to the opening of the Stainforth and Keadby Canal in 1797, the cut turves were carried down navigable drains that ran across the moors. After cutting the turf was dried on the areas of moor set aside for this with turves laid on the ground and built into heaps of twelve called 'walls' on Crowle Moors. The dry turves were then stacked in peat stacks called 'pyramids' until they were boated away.

However, it seems that the use of peat turf from the moors as fuel declined in the late 1700s and early 1800s. This was undoubtedly due to competition from collieries that were opening and supplying coal across the region but perhaps too to the requirement to pay dues on the new canal system. This decreased the economic competitiveness of the peat. However, the other factor that was coming into play was directly relevant to our story. The impact of drainage and then enclosure of the area was leading to the conversion of large amounts of former peat moor into arable land. The issue of peat cutting was in fact raised during the enclosure process. The 1811 Act for the Enclosure of Hatfield, Thorne and Fishlake stated that:

> no person was to pare, dig, cut, or take away any Wood, Turf, sods or soil of any part of the commons which were to be inclosed, until the allotments were made, although the 'Peat Moors', known by the Name of Thorne Waste, and which have Time immemorially been considered, used, and enjoyed as the Estate, Right and Property of the Person or Persons whose Estate abuts or adjoins the same, shall not be divided.

Indeed, in many ways it is this provision of the act which meant the fragments of the original Northern Fen today remaining as Thorne and Hatfield Moors survived at all. The rights of turbary in the part of Hatfield Chase within the Manor of Hatfield were to be reserved and the cutting and leading away of 'Turves from the peat or Turf Mosses' was to continue. However, this was to be for the use of local inhabitants only for domestic use and not for commercial sale. They were allowed to take the turf away in 'Carts, Waggons, and Carriages'.

With enclosure there was a new drain cut along the edge of Thorne Moors or Thorne Waste from Broadbentgate to the North Soak Drain. Like the other moorland drains this was used to carry small boats and loads of peat. However, in 1829 this was stopped because it was decided that 'boating was injurious to the drainage'. The extent of the navigable system of drains and dykes was quite significant; the main drains on the 1840s maps included at least six miles that could be navigated as boating dyke. But from around 1815 the turf trade dwindled and the remaining commercial activity supplied mostly Hull and York. There were only about eight or nine boats still operating and these were 'chiefly confined to the moors'. By 1837 White's directory reported that there were formerly about thirty boats operating but now only seven or eight, carrying to York, Hull, 'and other markets'. There are reports of peat turf used in metal working at sites close to Sheffield at about this time. Areas of the moors were being improved by warping. The land was drained, the top turf skimmed off, and then a deposit of silt was spread over the surface. This was either by manipulation of the tidal rivers or by carriage to the sites for spreading. In 1848 the Thorne Moor Drainage and Improvement Act established the Thorne Moor Improvement Company to reclaim the 'swampy bog'. In its establishment the company had capital of around £37,000 in £20 shares with a remit to improve small parts of the 'waste'. The process to be adopted was either a charge levied on private landowners for the service provided or to purchase the lands for the company itself. The process involved warping as already described and targeted areas in Fishlake, Hatfield, Thorne and Swinefleet. However, although these operations had local impacts on land use and water levels, they probably did not affect the overall integrity of the core peat mass and its high water-table. The Level of Hatfield Chase Act of 1862 may have resulted in some lowering of the water-table, but the central peat area still remained very wet.

As time progressed the gradual efforts from a number of players (the participants, the Improvement Company and individual private landowners) began to have an impact and agriculture began to squeeze out the now much smaller turf cutting industry. However, the potential business interests were changing and in 1854 EH Durden presented a paper to the Yorkshire Geological Society on 'the application of peat and its products to manufacturing, agricultural and sanitary purposes'. Now the peatland 'formerly a swampy bog' was becoming 'efficiently drained and prepared for improvement'.

There was a further twist, however. By the 1880s the market for peat moss as animal bedding to service needs in the army and especially in the rapidly spreading urban centres of Victorian England was to become the new big industry. The process of moorland reclamation was speeding up dramatically and a new industry was emerging. It was suggested that:

the moors have been developed in an extraordinary manner by the manipulation of the surface for peat moss litter which has now become a most important trade, the Thorne Moors finding employment for 350 hands in stripping the surface of the waste for litter. When the surface has been cleared, sluices made for the purpose are opened to admit the tidal water from the rivers Ouse and Don, which brings up rich earthy matter called 'warp' and deposits it on the land; by this treatment, pursued for about 3 years, extensive tracts of the waste have, since the beginning of the 19th century, been converted into fertile land of the most valuable kind. (Goodchild, 1971)

The history of the large-scale commercial exploitation of peat at Thorne Moors was described in detail by John Goodchild in 1971 and 1973, and then by Martin Limbert (1986). It is believed that the process began in earnest in around 1884 as a result of growing demand for peat litter for animal bedding, for warped land for agriculture and through the initiative of local business-minded people. By 1901 the Hatfield Chase Peat Moss Litter Company was working an irregular area with a series of parallel drainage channels and an access road over the Moors. This network of canals was imposed on the earlier landscape and not necessarily

Hand-Powered
Moss Litter
Machine

derived from the early system of drains, which had doubled up to provide water-borne transport. To give some indication of the emerging demands for peat moss litter, there was now nationally an increase of around 98,353 working horses between 1901 and 1906. These were employed by railways, tramways, omnibus companies, various local authority undertakings and of course many other businesses. Peat moss litter (dried peat) had been found to make an ideal bedding material for them. By the late 1890s the British Moss Litter Company was formed and took over a number of established peat works across the region between the Rivers Don and Trent. Alongside the system of canals and boats there was also developed a network of narrow gauge railways and connections beyond to the wide rail network. A new 'pressing mill' still known as the 'Paraffin Mill' or the 'Paraffin Works' was being built in 1895. This was to produce gas for fuel, ammonia water, paraffin, creosote, methyl alcohol, tar and even alcohol for motor cars. Peat dust was used to pack fruit and peat was even fed to cattle. However, these diversifications did not last long and the mill closed in 1922. With declining use of horses for industry and transport the moss litter business also collapsed. But by the 1930s and 1940s there emerged the interest in horticultural peat and it very nearly erased the entirety of the remaining Yorkshire Fens.

Chapter Nine

Conclusions: Climate-proofing a County
– Yorkshire's Fenlands and Flooding

The drainage of the fens and then the further 'improvement' of farmland in the wider landscape have major implications beyond just nature conservation and nostalgia. With the dramatic de-watering of the areas that provide the river catchments for these wetlands, such as the upland rivers in the Pennines for the Yorkshire Fens, the removal of lowland capacity to hold flood-water is catastrophic. In England and Wales around five million people live in areas at risk from flooding, and yet we seem perpet-ually surprised when we get wet. However, take a map of the flood risk areas and overlay a map of the land wrested by drainage and 'improvement' from the once great fenlands and the two are virtually the same. In the summer of 2007, first South Yorkshire and then the West Midlands experienced unprecedented damage and disruption with catastrophic floods in June and July. At the time a lot of reporting and many politicians stated that this was unusual and unexpected. I disagree. The floods were certainly extreme, and they were worse than most others of recent times, but history and science tell us that these are both predictable and they were predicted. What is more, a simple consideration of how we have managed the landscape in recent times suggests that these events should be expected, and with global climate change this will be more so in the future. Yet time and again we seem to be caught with our corporate trousers down and are terribly surprised. It is also very easy to find people to blame, and we live

155

in an increasingly blame-orientated society. Realistically today's politicians are not responsible for the long-term trends and circumstances that add up to disaster. A lack of critical and targeted investment in some aspects of infrastructure, and especially cuts in funds to key agencies, might fairly be laid at their door, but even that is only part of a longer-term neglect. Local politicians nationally may be guilty of development at any price – 'Sod the flood plain' – but then they always have been. What's new?

Discussions with politicians, media reporters and others suggest a reluctance to accept what happened as anything other than a one-off disaster rather than part of a long-term trend. Yet by the autumn of 2007 and the winter of 2008, the same areas affected by the summer floods were once again inundated. In January 2008 Andrew Wood, spokesperson for Natural England to the Defra select committee inquiry into flooding, stated that 'managing

Flooding June 2007

water naturally reduces flooding'. Not only this, but also that thriving wetlands, restored peat bogs and free-flowing rivers are recommended by Natural England to reduce the harmful effects of flooding. By increasing the natural capacity of the countryside to absorb and hold excess water, the risk of flooding could be dramatically decreased. This is exactly what I and others, notably Chris Baines, have been advocating for over ten years. Today, Chris Baines and others are campaigning for an extension to a 'whole landscape approach' and more woodland. In particular, they see a need for more woodland on the hillside and a reduction in the numbers of grazing animals in critical upland areas. Long-term, grant-aided policies have subsidized over-grazing of many moors and former bogs leading to soil compaction and reduced vegetation cover. Combined with publicly funded drainage of the same landscapes the results have been short-term boosts to productivity but totally unsustainable. We are now paying the penalty. Water that falls on such land runs off extremely quickly, potentially causing floods downstream.

The solution may involve the undoing of work of so-called 'land improvement' undertaken over many decades. There are other issues too and in particular the massive erosion of soil and sediments is worrying. This has an effect on the impacts of floodwaters downstream. However, there is a hidden menace too with the re-working and major re-distribution of toxic chemicals from a century or so of heavy industry. In catchments like the Rother in North Derbyshire and South Yorkshire, once the second most polluted river in Western Europe, pollutants such as lead, zinc, cadmium, mercury and dioxins were laid down within beds of sediments; a legacy of the wealth-creating industries of the nineteenth and twentieth centuries. Research at Sheffield Hallam University showed how the floods in the year 2000 scoured out the sediments to release the toxins downstream. The hope is that that the sheer volume of water has diluted the impacts. However, this is not known for certain, but it is clear that very nasty chemicals have been re-released and have ended up somewhere downstream. Other problems are the sheer volume of flood-driven erosion carrying sediment down into the lower catchments. This may add to the damage caused as sediment-loaded waters hit the flood risk zones. This isn't new. Prehistoric forest clearance caused massive downwash of soil and sediment from, for example, the Pennines into the low-lying rivers such as the Trent, the Ouse, and even across the extensive Lincolnshire Fens. This same erosion now causes catastrophic damage to heritage landscapes, in parts of Yorkshire eroding important archaeological sites as swollen rivers rip through the landscape. Archaeology that has survived a thousand years can be lost in a few hours.

Another problem that seems to be overlooked is the potential spread of invasive alien species, particularly Japanese knotweed, giant hogweed and Himalayan balsam, but also various aquatic invaders. There is much talk of 'whole catchment approaches' to management of invasives, but in truth very little action. Recent floods are now spreading propagules of these species far and wide across the lowland fens, so we can expect an exponential increase in the problem over the next few years. They all thrive on disturbance, the floods bring that with a vengeance, and the potential long-term costs of remedial management will be enormous.

Lessons of History

History, both recent and further back in time, tells us that flooding is not a new phenomenon. Accounts since biblical times have told stories of floods and of terrible storms. It seems strange therefore to view recent events as somehow unusual or unexpected; extreme, yes, but unexpected, no. There have even been major tsunamis in Britain, with a massive series of tidal waves striking eastern Scotland around 7,000 years ago, and then one around the Severn Estuary in the 1700s. There have always been storms and tempests and people have always suffered. Indeed, not only have floods and flood risk always been with us, but our management and use of the landscape, now combined with climate change, make them more rather than less likely. Some of this is actually very hard to prove beyond doubt in a scientifically testable way. However, observation of trends, a triangulation of findings and plain common sense leave little doubt as to what is happening. There is a degree of denial in certain quarters. Yet even a cursory dip into history and a sifting through newspapers over the last 200 years produces a vast array of examples of flood and storm catastrophes. Whilst coastal flooding has different causes and raises other issues, some of the context is the same. Again, a brief historic survey reveals the same location being affected time and again. Holmfirth, for example, suffered severe floods in 1738 and 1777, and then in 1852 there was the famous Holmfirth Flood when Bilberry Reservoir burst its dam and eighty-one lives were lost. But floods struck again in 1944 with further loss of life and extensive damage to property. The 1852 flood followed heavy rain but it was linked to reported construction defects in the reservoir. The torrent of waves crashed through Holmfirth and on as far as Lockwood, near Huddersfield. York is regularly inundated, but over the

Floods

decades Malton, Doncaster, Sheffield, Hull and many others have also suffered.

It is always suggested that each flood results from un-precedented and unusual weather, a case of an 'extreme event', so how many unusual and infrequent events must we experience before they are accepted as increasingly the norm? In Yorkshire, for example, we had floods in York and Thirsk in November 2000, Helmsley in June 2005, Leeds and Harrogate in September 2006 and South Yorkshire and Ryedale in July 2007. This suggests these are not so unusual. They are extreme, but with climate change extreme becomes commonplace. Climate manifested in the weather is changing, getting more extreme, both hot and dry, or, as we witnessed in 2007, bringing torrential deluges of rain. The autumn of 2000 was the wettest for 270 years; the associated flooding affected 10,000 properties. In January 2005 there were floods affecting around 3,000 properties, with a similar figure for June and July 2007. With global climate change now accepted fact, although we can debate the exact causes, it has been calculated that the associated costs of flood damage might be £25 billion per year, an increase from the present £1 billion. These are the raw figures that disguise even greater worries and costs.

Landscape Change

There are other factors too, in particular the way people have changed the landscape over the centuries. Over hundreds of years, but increasingly during the late twentieth century, we have changed the environment in which we live, work and recreate. Urban areas have sprawled out over floodplains, turning soft, porous surfaces to tarmac and concrete. But there is more: our impacts have not been restricted to the built environment; we have drained and 'improved' huge areas of farmland. Drainage was an obsession of the Victorians. From the highest parts of the Pennines, the North York Moors, the eastern Peak District and the Yorkshire Wolds with their 'gripping', to the lowlands of the Vale of York, the flatlands of Doncaster, Pickering and Holderness, the story is the same: drain, drain and drain.

Agricultural Drainage

Farmers have been driven by government polices over decades, by massive subsidies from EU and UK governments and by public demand for evermore cheap food. This probably peaked in the 1970s at around 100,000 hectares drained per year. Whilst the trend has largely halted, any reversion has been very piecemeal and relatively modest. This was especially the case in flood risk areas such as the Vale of Pickering, Holderness, the Vale of York, the Rother Valley, the Don Valley and similar landscapes throughout the county. In other areas, localized but significant, the riverbank has been sacrificed to urban city heartlands and industry. If this was not enough, in recent years we began to build anew on former expansive floodplains, the natural control systems of Britain's lowland landscapes. We have also removed woods and trees from the landscape over many centuries and many wooded or plantation sites today are also extensively drained. This is analogous to the grips of upland moors, but is almost totally overlooked. Anyone involved in Forestry Commission schemes from the 1950s to the 1990s will tell you about the extent and scale of drainage involved. All this removes capacity to hold water and to slow its movement through the landscape.

The Catchment of the Yorkshire Fens

England's third-largest fenland, bordering North Lincolnshire, Nottinghamshire and South Yorkshire, was almost totally destroyed by the early 1900s by the long-term impact of intensive land management and the drainage efforts of the Dutch engineers. The consequences and impacts of these changes were discussed earlier. In South Yorkshire before the drainage of 36,420 hectares of the Humberhead Levels the area was 'A continual lake and a rondezvous of ye waters of ye rivers . . . ' (de la Pryme, 1699). However, this is only the lower part of the catchment. In the upper zone, the high Pennine moors, there has been massive peat fuel removal and associated drainage. This has been followed by intensive farming of sheep and grouse with associated gripping. The Dark Peak, from which a massive amount of peat has been removed, is surrounded by valleys now famous for their water-supply reservoirs. The removal of peat, conservatively estimated to be around 34 million cubic metres from the Dark Peak plateaux, undoubtedly has a major impact on the water-holding capacity of this catchment. In water supply terms, this has been calculated as the equivalent to the loss of a reservoir containing 340 billion litres (or 75 billion gallons). The water storage capacity of peat is prodigious. For example, ombrotrophic *Sphagnum* peat can hold 500–600 per cent water on a dry weight basis, whilst peat on average contains 5.5 gallons per cubic foot. The region is illustrated below to show the macro-linkage between upper and lower catchments. These are joined by landscapes of urban development and often of industry or intensive agriculture. Over around three centuries this landscape has been transformed from being dominated by heath, moor, woodland, unimproved pasture, marsh and fen from the high ground to the coastal lowlands.

Coastal zones along Holderness and around the Humber pose particular problems with regard to storms, floods and erosion. In general they are exposed to major storm or tidal impacts and obviously extremely vulnerable to sea level rise. In Britain there is the particular problem of coastal subsidence and erosion, and hence exacerbated flood risk. However, a major reason for the concern about coastal areas is simply because we have reclaimed large areas of productive land from the sea, but they may no longer be sustainable. Hull is itself built on reclaimed coastal flats and lies downstream of huge areas of improved upland sheep walk and drained valley fens: there is little excuse for surprise when the floodwaters rise again.

Climate, Weather and Floods

Weather and climate clearly influence flood risk and storm damage in many, though not all, situations. However, the relationships and trends are not simple. In addressing the problems and issues it is important to recognize that flood and drought are flipsides of the same issue. A flood today does not diminish the chances of a drought tomorrow. It is clear that the 'the rules of engagement' between people, weather and landscape have changed. In the future we will need to plan in order to absorb the effects of a more extreme climate, and this extends not just to infrastructure and engineering but to the wider landscape too. Landscape change has clearly generated some flooding problems and at the very least it has exacerbated the risks through bad weather and through development-related impacts.

However, there is now a cost for the changes that we have imposed upon the landscape and it is payback time. With our rivers straightened and canalized, they are now locked into artificial banks, and the natural drainage systems are de-coupled from their floodplains. The latter are massively reduced or totally removed. Rivers are mostly lined by intensive farming, which grew rapidly from the 1950s to the 1990s. To add to the problems, our increasingly extreme weather is dumping unbelievable quantities of water on to vulnerable areas, and in short, intensive periods. As we experienced in 2007, though, the heavy rain is coming in the midst of longer, persistent rainy periods. Consequently the 'natural' landscape can't cope and the built structures are at their limits or beyond. With what we've done, this is hardly surprising.

There is a further worry for those living or working in many of the lower-lying coastal zones and the extensive flatlands of the Northern Fens: the threat of climate-induced sea level rise. Yorkshire around Hull and Holderness includes areas already at or even below sea level. This is a serious menace in decades to come, and of course the south-eastern seaboard of Britain is also slowly sinking anyway. A combination of a North Sea surge, as happened in 1953, but more recently without incident in autumn 2007, and inland rainfall as experienced in South Yorkshire in summer 2007 could be devastating. With ever-increasing urban development in these areas as well, the hydrology is compromised and people and property are increasingly at risk. There is a huge and growing literature on this topic with extensive and deeply researched assessments and guidance. Yet despite all this discussion and research, the problem is yet to be solved. There was a massive surge along the East Coast in November 2007. It did not breech but it was within a few inches of doing so. For all those lands across the Yorkshire Fens which now lie below sea level this still remains a massive threat, as it did back in the 1200s or the 1500s. It many ways, though, the situation has worsened. As the earlier writers described the shrinkage of the fenland soils and in the 1940s war effort the topsoils simply blowing away, our engineered solutions have shrunk the land. More and more land lies lower and lower and sea level is rising. The barriers and embankments have generally held in recent years, but there is a real risk with floodwater in that water will always find the lowest point and will flow that way. You only need one breech, one failure to place a huge area at risk.

Flood Risk and Positive Planning

However, it is not just in the coastal zone that people are now at risk. Across huge areas of landscape the natural wetlands have been removed and replaced by intensive farming, by industry and commerce, and often by housing. In South Yorkshire alone ninety-nine per cent of England's third-biggest fenland has been destroyed, and most moorland removed or drained, much funded by the public purse. There are now pioneering developments such as the RPSB Old Moor Nature Reserve in the Dearne Valley and the Potteric Carr Nature Reserve in Doncaster that are beginning to help reinvigorate this landscape. But whilst these major new wetlands helped lessen recent flood impacts, they are not enough.

So what must we now do? To solve the problems, especially if climate change accelerates, as seems likely, we need radical, far-reaching actions that place a new emphasis on the importance of fenlands and the fens. They need to address wider issues across entire catchments beyond the flood risk areas, making sustainable drainage systems compulsory for major new developments and going beyond flood protection. It is not enough to demand an absence of a negative impact on flood risk in a floodplain. In future it will be necessary to ensure that all developments make positive contributions to water management, or else planning permission should be refused. Obviously this applies mainly to larger developments, but all housing and business premises can make a contribution across the whole catchment. This need not be draconian or prohibitively expensive: for smaller premises simply including soft and porous surfaces, and perhaps where appropriate soakaways, would be sufficient.

The years to come will undoubtedly see massive investment in the engineered infrastructure that manages water and combats floods. This will include barriers, embankments, upgraded drainage systems and the rest, costing millions of pounds. The story of our lost Yorkshire Fens documents the same approach over at least a thousand years and we still have problems. So it seems the evidence is that it has not been a total success. At the same time, though, there is still the threat of further development on the floodplain, nature's water management system. So we are essentially working *against* the grain of nature and not *with* it. The human suffering and individual dilemmas then kick in, and those at risk may be trapped and unable to move. Realistically, after all that has happened, who is going to move *into* a flood risk zone? If willing buyers are found, then they surely will not pay the market prices that would have been expected prior to the latest floods. House values and saleability will fall. To compound the suffering, there are serious questions about whether home-owners will be able to get, or at least afford, flood damage insurance. Again, if they cannot, then in future fewer people will risk living in flood zones. This is a controversial issue, since although the intensity of recent events has been surprising the catastrophes that resulted were to a degree predictable. We have suffered major floods and storm damage since time immemorial, and historic records document these back over a thousand years. Indeed, whilst individual incidents cannot be reliably forecast, they were to an extent predicted by both environmentalists and planners. Planning reports back in the 1920s, for example, warned specifically against building on Yorkshire's floodplains in the old West Riding (including South Yorkshire). This, along with similar advice given ever since, was largely ignored. We know that building on flood plains is a bad idea, but we go ahead because it is easy to do. There are both immense short-term financial gains for developers and landowners, and these are coupled with acute housing shortage and huge pressure for new developments. The local authorities are charged with protecting communities against flooding but also with providing enough new homes – the horns of a dilemma. In some localized areas it may make sense to help residents move to new, safer locations rather than continuing to face a losing battle with the elements. This may not be what people wish to hear and it will be a hard truth to bear. However, the principle has already been established in terms of the abandonment of active protection of some coastal zones that are at risk and now considered indefensible. However, here again I would argue that there may be a difference between regrouping our defences strategically and realigning to beyond a coastal zone that was relatively recently reclaimed from the sea, and wholesale abandonment of eroding shorelines along the east coast. With rising sea levels and increasingly powerful storms, erosion potential will increase. Chris Smout has recently reported from Scotland the massive increase and catastrophic impacts of storm erosion events along the northern coastlines. There is the question for those living and working in the fenland regions, and in coastal zones from Holderness to Suffolk, of how far are we prepared to step back from defending a line. At what point will we decide to stop the eroding coasts and how much are we prepared to accept the losses and over what timescale? This book is about human interaction with nature and the assumption often that we have the power to control it. Accepting that we cannot totally control nature and that it would be undesirable to do so does not necessarily mean that we can afford to abrogate responsibility. It is perhaps one thing to state that we will allow the sea to retake Holderness, to the point of a few hundred metres in the next twenty-five years, even with the drastic impacts on the relatively few people affected. However, are we really prepared over the next hundred years or so to lose entire towns such as Hornsea, Withernsea, and even Great Driffield or Beverley in Holderness? The potential loss in terms of landscape, of archaeology, of wildlife, and, increasingly important in a global context of food security, of productive farmland, seems massive. At the same time, exactly how much of the vast areas of the inland of the Northern Fens are we really prepared to now abandon to the waters? These are serious issues and pertinent questions which raise matters of long-term strategies and visions. The present responses are short term and generally politically safe and accept-able, often determined by the limited tenure of governments and the increasingly short job tenure of a constantly fluctuating set of ever-changing agencies and the mobility of the officers between jobs and responsibilities. The story of *Yorkshire's Forgotten Fens* is the account of a long-term interaction with water and the water's edge. The next critical steps on this journey also require a long-term vision and commitment that we presently lack.

Effective Responses

The story of people and fens has been one of managing risk and benefit over centuries. The fenland peoples in the past generally knew what to expect with the seasons and they knew that the occasional catastrophe could happen. But living and working in the wetland or around the water's edge was a balance between the dangers and problems and the rich wealth that such an existence offered. The same applies today as it has always done. Indeed, with the increasing concerns over global food supplies and the competitive world markets, it is unlikely that much more prime arable land will be freely given up by farmers and landowners or by politicians. There will be a renewed interest in squeezing the last kilos of food production from the fenland landscapes. However, this will only exacerbate future flood and drought risks and solutions will need to be found even to maintain the productive system. In the short term, engineering will be a vital part of any effective response, to avoid system overload in drains and channels and to protect critically 'at risk' services such as power and water. This is only a part of the solution and not in itself a long-term, sustainable option. In many situations this is a case of treating the symptoms, not addressing the causes of the problems. It is what I call the sticking-plaster approach, and not curing the underlying problems of water management. In the short term, targeted engineering is all we have got, but we must now learn from recent experience. Furthermore, we must plan for even more extreme events to come. This means taking the threats seriously and planning accordingly, and long term.

Heron

We must learn to work with the grain of nature, not against it, and the main battlegrounds will be in the Yorkshire Fens, their catchments and the eastern seaboard. But what does this imply? On the one hand I suggest that appropriate sustainable drainage systems become mandatory on all new developments. These will vary with locations and with specific conditions, but the technology is there, it just needs to be applied. They include recent innovations such as green roofs. Again, this will not be enough, but only part of the solution. Like the boy with his finger in the dyke, we need something more sustainable, and the key players in a more secure future will be farmers. We need to work with and pay farmers, as custodians of the landscape, to manage their land to hold back the floodwaters. This will not be cheap, but it will cost less than the alternative of repeated damage and disruption and the continued distress and suffering of home owners and other across the region. To remediate the damage of centuries of environmental degradation, the longer-term solution must be landscape scale and centred around those who manage the landscape: our farmers. In this context, in recent years there has been much talk about how farmers are custodians of the countryside and that they should be rewarded for this role. It is time to deliver on such talk. Changes in EU funding to Single Farm Payments and Environmental Stewardship are moves in the right direction and towards broader outputs rather than just food production. However, it still seems there is a gulf between policy, need and action, and as stated earlier this must be genuinely long term and visionary, and not the prevailing way, which is to avoid the key issues and to fudge the responses.

Importantly too, with an increasingly urban population often disengaged from the farming world, there remain serious problems in getting the effective message across. It is surely no coincidence that recent years have seen many families going out of farming after generations on the land and serious difficulties in recruiting new people to the industry. Ask any agricultural college and you will be told a tale of falling numbers coming to train in mainstream agriculture. One of the principal problems seems to be in recognizing the central role of farming in delivering on the issues and outcomes high on political and popular agendas. There is much written, and there are endless policies, on sustainability, on responses to climate change and on quality of life, and even rural renaissance. But one struggles to find how farmers and land managers are identified in these as the core group of people tasked with delivery. They are not. It seems that neither the farming industry and community nor the wider public have grasped the fact that it is land managers who must deliver a more sustainable future. To do this requires vision, skills and a vibrant community of professionals, including farmers and foresters. The issues range from changing farm practice and all the hotly debated matters of carbon footprints and offset but also the more tangible things such as the management of water and the sustainable production of good-quality food. So here's the rub. What has happened to all the talk of paying the farmer to manage the flood? What happened to proposals to extend woodland cover to help mop up excess water? When York was badly hit a few years ago, and then areas around the Severn Valley were also affected, it was said that the solution was, at least in part, to pay the land manager for an ecosystem service. We can even calculate a monetary 'worth' of such services with a toolkit provided by the former Office of the Deputy Prime Minister, but the necessary steps simply are not happening. It is clearly possible to target major landscape change both positively and quickly, when we want to.

Planning for Sustainable Solutions

Each storm and every flood is a sexy media event, but once it has passed the spotlight shifts. Bodies such as the RSPB and Natural England are now pushing on with big proposals to create large wetlands in coastal zones and inland areas. These are exciting projects, but will still not be enough. A long-term sustainable solution will need to be bigger and even more radical. This needs to be at a wider catchment scale, to address opportunities both large and small for positive water management. Some of this involves a critical look at planning zones and procedures. There should be no more floodplain developments unless absolute need is demonstrated. But beyond this, all significant new developments, whether on the floodplain or not, should guarantee a positive impact on water management. This is a shift from the idea of simply demonstrating the absence of a negative impact to positive management for water. The location of critical infrastructure should, where possible, not be sited within a floodplain, or if it is, then measures should be adopted to offset floodwater elsewhere close by. The approach needs to include innovative developments such as green roofs (with living vegetation to hold rainwater back), soakaways (to help rain be absorbed into the groundwater from developments), swales (which hold back floodwaters on rivers and streams) and porous surfaces (for example for roads and pavements) as the rule and not the exception. However, it also needs to address the 1.3 million hectares of agricultural land in England and Wales that are on floodplains and the extensive areas of woodlands and plantations too. Here the Northern Fens are both most at risk but also present the greatest opportunities.

In the wider catchment there needs to be a long-term programme of environmental re-construction to remediate for decades and even centuries of damage. This cannot be achieved overnight, but there are signs of things moving in the right direction. From Peak District moorland restoration to lowland fen re-creation, there are projects that can begin to halt the damage. Tree and woodland management will also be a part of this bigger picture. We know that at a catchment scale trees and woods can help moderate water behaviour and we need to harness this knowledge to enhance sustainable water management. We also know that trees can moderate the excesses of climate change at a local urban level, perhaps moderating summer temperature highs by several degrees. Perhaps riverine floodplain woodlands will have a role to play as well in holding water back and helping to reduce sediment burden in floodwater. Alongside any woodland re-establishment there will need to be a programme of restoration of bogs and marshes, again to hold back and slow down the floodwaters. This will include targeted re-construction of both long-term wetter landscapes and new areas for floodwater storage when the need arises. Part of what needs to be done is the restoration of an old landscape. However, this should not be undertaken as an exercise in looking back, except perhaps to learn from mistakes. What is now needed is a new and clear vision that can engage stakeholders from the public and home owners, to the wider landowners and managers and developers, to politicians, agencies and the media. This is essential because decisions need to be better informed, to be responsive to change and accountable to those affected. The changes need to be approached in a positive way to create new opportunities rather than barriers. A wetter landscape will provide water as a sustainable resource, new farming opportunities, new and extensive recreation and tourism opportunities and economic benefits, and it will provide ecosystem services of flood management, biodiversity and carbon sequestration. This will not be easy and it does not imply the abandonment of agriculture, of development or of flood control engineering. All these lie at the core of the vision, but they are placed in a context of long-term sustainable development. This is something that we hear a lot about and now is the time to deliver. Only time will tell. So until the next time the waters rise . . .

Bibliography and References

Anon. (1820). *The History and Antiquities of Thorne with Some Account of the Drainage of Hatfield Chase*. Thorne: S Whaley.

Anon. (1997). *The Humberhead Peatlands National Nature Reserve on the South Yorkshire/North Lincolnshire border*. Wakefield: English Nature.

Anon. (undated). *The Humberhead: Turning the Tide of History*. Wakefield: English Nature.

Allen, T (1828). *A New and Complete History of the County of York*. I T Hinton, London.

Allison, K J (1976). *The East Riding of Yorkshire Landscape*. London: Hodder & Stoughton.

Bain, C and Eversham, B C, eds (1991). *Thorne & Hatfield Moors Papers*, 2. Doncaster: Thorne & Hatfield Moors Conservation Forum.

Bain, C and Eversham, B C, eds (1992). *Thorne & Hatfield Moors Papers*, 3. Doncaster: Thorne & Hatfield Moors Conservation Forum.

Blashill, T (1900). *Sutton-in-Holderness: The Manor, the Berewic and the Village Community*. London: Elliot Stock.

Buckland, P C (1979). *Thorne Moors: A Palaeoecological Study of a Bronze Age Site: A Contribution to the History of the British Insect Fauna*. Birmingham: Department of Geography Occasional Publication 8, University of Birmingham.

Buckland, P C and Dinnin, M H (1997). The Rise and Fall of a Wetland Habitat: Recent Palaeoecological Research on Thorne and Hatfield Moors. *Thorne & Hatfield Moors Papers*, 4. Doncaster: Thorne & Hatfield Moors Conservation Forum: 1–18.

Bunting, W (1983). *An Outline Study of the Level of Hatfield Chase, Part Three*. Thorne: Wm Bunting.

Butlin, R A, ed (2003). *Historical Atlas of North Yorkshire*. Otley: Westbury.

Caufield, C (1991). *Thorne Moors*. St Albans: Sumach Press.

Clarke, E (1887). Potterick Carr. *The Field*, 26 November.

Cobbett, W (1853). *Rural Rides*. Expanded edition of the 1830 issue with appendices. London.

Cornish, C J (1895). *Wild England Today*. London: Seeley.

Cory, V (1985). *Hatfield and Axholme: An Historical Review*. Ely: Providence Press.

Credland, A G, ed (1998). *Burton Constable Hall: The Eighteenth and Nineteenth Centuries*. Beverley: East Yorkshire Local History Society.

Darby, H C and Maxwell, I S, eds (1962). *The Domesday Geography of Northern England*. Cambridge: Cambridge University Press.

de la Pryme, A (1870). *The Diary of Abraham de La Pryme: The Yorkshire Antiquary*. Durham: Andrews.

de la Pryme (1699), letters as quoted in Dinnin, M (1997). The Drainage History of the Humberhead Levels. In R Van de Noort and S Ellis, *Wetland Heritage of the Humberhead Levels: An Archaeological Survey*. Hull: Humber Wetlands Project, University of Hull.

Defoe, D (1724–1726). *A Tour Through England and Wales*. London.

Dinnin, M (1997). The Drainage History of the Humberhead Levels. In R Van de Noort and S Ellis, *Wetland Heritage of the Humberhead Levels: An Archaeological Survey*. Hull: Humber Wetlands Project, University of Hull.

Dugdale, W (1772[2]). *The History of Imbanking and Draining of Divers Fens and Marshes, both in Foreign Parts and in this Kingdom, and of the Improvements thereby*. Revised and corrected by Charles Nalson Cole. London: W Bowyer and F Nichols.

Dunston, G (1912). *The Rivers of Axholme with a History of the Navigable Rivers and Canals of the District*. London: A Brown & Sons.

English, B (1990). *The Great Landowners of East Yorkshire 1530–1910*. Howden: Hull Academic Press.

Eversham, B C (1991). Thorne and Hatfield Moors: Implications of Land Use Change for Nature Conservation. *Thorne & Hatfield Moors Papers*, 2. Doncaster: Thorne & Hatfield Moors Conservation Forum: 3–18.

Firth, C (1997). *900 Years of the Don Fishery: Domesday to the Dawn of the New Millennium*. Leeds: Environment Agency.

Garnett, A (1961). From Pennine High Peak to the Humber. In J Mitchell, ed, *Great Britain Geographical Essays*. London: Cambridge University Press.

Gelling, M (1984). *Place-Names in the Landscape*. London: Phoenix Press.

Gelling, M and Cole, A (2000). *The Landscape of Place-Names*. Stamford: Shaun Tyas.

Giblett, R (1996). *Postmodern Wetlands: Culture, History, Ecology*. Edinburgh: Edinburgh University Press.

Goodchild, J, ed (1971). 'The Peat-cutting Industry of South Yorkshire.' *The South Yorkshire Journal*, part three, May 1971: 1–5.

Goodchild, J, ed (1973). 'The Peat-cutting Industry of South Yorkshire: Part Two.' *The South Yorkshire Journal*, part four, April 1973: 11–19.

Grindell, D W (2008). Beverley's 'Carpenter's Yards' (1756–1956) and the Story of the Last Wooden Keel: The Evolution of Beverley Beck Navigation and East Yorkshire Drainage. *East Yorkshire Local History Society Series* 56. Beverley: East Yorkshire Local History Society.

Gurney, J H (1921). *Early Annals of Ornithology*. London: H F & G Witherby.

Haggard, H Rider (1902). *Rural England: Being an Account of Agricultural and Social Researches Carried Out in the Years 1901 & 1902*. London: Longmans, Green, volume 2.

Harris, L E (1953). *Vermuyden and the Fens: A Study of Sir Cornelius Vermuyden and the Great Level*. London: Cleaver-Hume Press.

Harrison, K and Rotherham, I D (2007). A Memory Re-discovered of South Yorkshire's Fens: Map-based Reconstruction of the Region's Former Wetlands. *The Yorkshire Naturalists' Union Bulletin* 48: 1–8.

Hogan, D V and Maltby, E (2005). *The Potential for Carbon Sequestration in Wetlands of the Humberhead Levels*. London: Technical Report, Royal Holloway Institute for Environmental Research, Royal Holloway University of London.

Jeffrys (1772), *Map of the County of Yorkshire*. Lympne: Harry Margary (1973).

Johnstone, J (1801²). *An Account of the Mode of Draining Land, According to the System Practised by Mr Joseph Elkington*. London: Board of Agriculture.

Jones, M (1996). Deer in South Yorkshire: An Historical Perspective. In M Jones, I D Rotherham and A J McCarthy, eds, Deer or the New Woodlands? *The Journal of Practical Ecology and Conservation, Special Publication* 1. Sheffield: Wildtrack.

Kerridge, E (1973). *The Farmers of Old England*. London: George Allen & Unwin.

Korthals-Altes, J (1925). *Sir Cornelius Vermuyden*. London and The Hague: Williams & Norgate and W P Van Stockum & Son.

Limbert, M (1986). The Exploitation of Peat at Thorne. *Old West Riding* 6 (1): 9–16.

Limbert, M, Mitchell, R D and Rhodes, R J (1986). *Thorne Moors Birds and Man*. Doncaster: Doncaster & District Ornithological Society.

Limbert, M, ed (1987a). *Thorne & Hatfield Moors Papers* 1. Doncaster: Doncaster Naturalists' Society.

Limbert, M (1987b). Some Notes on the Landscape History of Thorne Moors. *Thorne & Hatfield Moors Papers* 1: 31–43.

Limbert, M and Eversham, B C, eds (1997). *Thorne & Hatfield Moors Papers* 4. Doncaster: Thorne & Hatfield Moors Conservation Forum.

Limbert, M, ed (1998a). *Thorne & Hatfield Moors Papers* 5. Doncaster: Thorne & Hatfield Moors Conservation Forum.

Limbert, M, ed (1998b). *Thorne & Hatfield Moors Papers* 5. Doncaster: Thorne & Hatfield Moors Conservation Forum.

Limbert, M (2002). *The Mechanisation of Peat Winning on Thorne Moors*. Doncaster: Technical Report 8, Thorne & Hatfield Moors Conservation Forum.

Limbert, M and Roworth, P C (2009[2]). *The Mechanised Peat Winning and Transportation on Thorne Moors*. Doncaster: Technical Report 8, Thorne & Hatfield Moors Conservation Forum.

Lindley, K (1982). *Fenland Riots and the English Revolution*. London: Heinemann.

Long, W H (1969). *A Survey of the Agriculture of Yorkshire*. London: Royal Agricultural Society of England.

Lunn, D (1993). *Kings, Canals and Coal: Some Account of the Parishes in and around Hatfield Chace. History and Topography of Parishes of the Diocese of Sheffield*. Sheffield: Tenfold, volume 2.

Lythe, S G E (1938). Drainage and Reclamation in Holderness and the River Hull Valley, 1760–1880. *Geography* 23: 237–249.

Lythe, S G E (1939). The Organisation of Drainage and Embankment in Mediaeval Holderness. *Yorkshire Archaeological Journal* 1939: 282–295.

Marshall, W (1796). *The Rural Economy of Yorkshire*. London: G Nicol, 2 volumes.

Marshall, W (1808). *The Review and Abstract of the County Reports to the Board of Agriculture. Volume 1: Northern Department*. London: Longman, Hurst, Rees, Orme and Brown.

Martins, S W (2004). *Farmers, Landlords and Landscapes. Rural Britain, 1720 to 1870*. Macclesfield: Windgather Press.

Menuge, N J (2003). Drainage and Wetland Sites in the Vale of Pickering. In R A Butlin, ed, *Historical Atlas of North Yorkshire*. Otley: Westbury: 157–158.

Milsom, T, ed (2006). *Land Use, Ecology and Conservation in the Lower Derwent Valley.* York.

Parker, D J and Penning-Rowsell, E C (1980). *Chesil Sea Defence Scheme: Benefit Assessment.* Middlesex Polytechnic.

Peck, W (1813). *A Topographical History and Description of Bawtry and Thorne with the Villages Adjacent.* Doncaster: Thomas and Hunsley.

Peck, W (1815). *A Topographical Account of the Isle of Axholme, being the West Division of the Wapentake of Manley, in the County of Lincoln.* Doncaster: Thomas and Hunsley.

Purseglove, J (1988). *Taming the Flood: A History and Natural History of Rivers and Wetlands.* Oxford: Oxford University Press.

Rackham, O (1986). *The History of the Countryside.* London: J M Dent & Sons.

Rimington, E (1992). Butterflies of the Doncaster District. *Sorby Record Special Series* 9.

Rippon, S (2000). *The Transformation of Coastal Wetlands.* Oxford: The British Academy, Oxford University Press.

Rotherham, I D and Harrison, K (2006). History and Ecology in the Reconstruction of the South Yorkshire Fens: Past, Present and Future. In B Davies and S Thompson, eds, *Water and the Landscape: The Landscape Ecology of Freshwater Ecosystems.* Oxford: IALE UK, Proceedings of the IALE Conference: 8–16.

Rotherham, I D (2008a). Floods and Water: A Landscape-scale Response. In I D Rotherham, ed, *Flooding, Water and the Landscape.* Sheffield: Wildtrack: 128–137.

Rotherham, I D (2008b). Landscape, Water and History. In I D Rotherham, ed, *Flooding, Water and the Landscape.* Sheffield: Wildtrack: 138–152.

Saxton, C (1577). *Map of the County of Yorkshire.*

Saxton, C and Goodman, W (1616). *Map Of Pottrick Carr near Doncaster.* Local Archives, Doncaster MBC Libraries.

Sheppard, J (1957). The Medieval Meres of Holderness. *Transactions of the Institute of British Geographers* XXIII: 75–86.

Sheppard, J (1958). The Draining of the Hull Valley. *East Yorkshire Local History Series* 8. Beverley: East Yorkshire Local History Society.

Sheppard, J (1966). The Draining of the Marshlands of South Holderness and the Vale of York. *East Yorkshire Local History Series* 20. Beverley: East Yorkshire Local History Society.

Skempton, A W, ed (1981). *John Smeaton FRS.* London: Thomas Telford.

Skidmore, P, Limbert, M and Eversham, B C (1985). The Insects of Thorne Moors. *Sorby Record* 23: supplement.

Skidmore, P (1992). Balaam's Donkey and the Hairy Canary: Personal Reflections on the Changing Invertebrates of Thorne and Hatfield Moors. *Thorne & Hatfield Moors Papers* 3: 66–70.

Smith, R (2004). *Enjoying the Humberhead Levels*. Tiverton: Halsgrove.

Smith, R, ed (2004). *The Marsh of Time: Saving Sutton Common*. Tiverton: Halsgrove.

Smout, C (2000). *Nature Contested: Environmental History in Scotland and Northern England since 1600*. Edinburgh: Edinburgh University Press.

Smiles, S (1904). *Lives of the Engineers*. London: John Murray.

Strong, R (1996). *The Story of Britain*. London: Hutchinson.

Taylor, M (1987). *Thorne Mere and the Old River Don*. Ebor Press.

Thompson, P (1856). *History and Antiquities of Boston*. London and Boston: John Noble Junior, Longman.

Tomlinson, J (1882). *The Level of Hatfield Chace and Parts Adjacent*. Doncaster: John Tomlinson.

Tuke, J (1800). *General View of the Agriculture of the North Riding of Yorkshire*. London: B McMillan.

Van de Noort, R and Davies, P (1993). *Wetland Heritage: An Archaeological Assessment of the Humber Wetlands*. Hull: Humber Wetlands Project, University of Hull.

Van de Noort, R and Ellis, S (1997). *Wetland Heritage of the Humberhead Levels: An Archaeological Survey*. Hull: Humber Wetlands Project, University of Hull.

Van de Noort, R (2001). *Thorne Moors: A Contested Wetland in North-Eastern England*. In B Coles and A Olivier, eds, *The Heritage Management of Wetlands In Europe*. Brussels: EAC: 133–140.

Van de Noort, R (2004). *The Humber Wetlands: The Archaeology of a Dynamic Landscape*. Macclesfield: Windgather Press.

Vermuyden, C (1626). *Map of Hatfield Chace before the Drainage*.

Whitehouse, N J, Dinnin, M H and Lindsay, R A (1998). Conflicts between Palaoecology, Archaeology and Nature Conservation: The Humberhead Peatlands SSSI. In I D Rotherham and M Jones, eds, *Landscapes: Perception, Recognition and Management: Reconciling the Impossible?* Proceedings of the Conference held in Sheffield, UK, 2–4 April. *Landscape Archaeology and Ecology* 3: 70–78.

Wilcox, H A (1933). *The Woodlands and Marshlands of England*. London: University Press of Liverpool, Hodder & Stoughton.

Woodruffe-Peacock, E A (1920-1921). The Ecology of Thorne Waste. *The Naturalist* 45: 301-304, 353-356, 381-384; 46: 21-25.

Woodward, D, ed (1985). Descriptions of East Yorkshire: Leland to Defoe. *East Yorkshire Local History Series* 39. Beverley: East Yorkshire Local History Society.

Young, A (1772). *Political Essays*. London: W Strahan and T Cadell, reprint 1970, New York: Research Reprints.

Index